Taking Off
Workbook
Second Edition

Susan Hancock Fesler   Christy M. Newman
Workbook Writer: Mari Vargo

McGraw-Hill

Taking Off Beginning English Workbook, 2nd Edition

Published by McGraw-Hill ESL/ELT, a business unit of The McGraw-Hill Companies, Inc., 1221 Avenue of the Americas, New York, NY 10020. Copyright © 2008 by The McGraw-Hill Companies, Inc. All rights reserved. No part of this publication may be reproduced or distributed in any form or by any means, or stored in a database or retrieval system, without the prior written consent of The McGraw-Hill Companies, Inc., including, but not limited to, in any network or other electronic storage or transmission, or broadcast for distance learning.

ISBN 10: 0-07-331437-4
ISBN 13: 978-0-07-331437-2
3 4 5 6 7 8 9 QPD 11 10 09

Project manager: Linda O'Roke
Cover designer: Wee Design
Interior designer: Aptara
Artists: Mick Reid, Roberta Rieple

Cover Art by Anna Divito

To the Teacher

Taking Off is a four-skills, standards-based program for beginning students of English. Picture dictionary art pages teach life-skills vocabulary in a clear and visual way. The gradually accelerating pace of the book instills confidence in students as they establish a solid foundation in the basics of English.

The *Taking Off* Workbook provides supplementary practice for students who have basic reading and writing skills in their first language. Each *Taking Off* Workbook unit provides 12 pages of supplementary activities for its corresponding Student Book unit. The Workbook activities offer students further practice in developing the language, vocabulary, and life-skill competencies taught in the Student Book. Answers to the Workbook activities are available in the *Taking Off* Teacher's Edition.

Features

- **NEW** *Grammar* activities provide further practice with the grammar taught in each unit.

- **NEW** *Reading* activities reuse and recycle vocabulary and grammar in new contexts as students practice finding the main idea and other comprehension skills.

- **NEW** *Writing* activities provide structured writing experiences that encourage students to personalize the vocabulary and grammar they have learned in the unit.

- **NEW** **Go online!** *Go online!* activities give students the opportunity to search the Internet using personal information and vocabulary taught in each unit.

- **Wide range of activities** can be used by students working independently or in groups, in the classroom, with a tutor, or at home.

- **New cast of characters** represents the same nationalities as the characters in the Student Book, but lends the Workbook a fresh set of faces.

- *Just for Fun* pages at the end of each unit feature word searches, crossword puzzles, and word scrambles.

- **Student Book page references** at the top of each Workbook page show how the two components support one another.

- **Correlation table at the back of the Workbook** helps teachers quickly cross-reference the Workbook and the Student Book.

The *Taking Off* Workbook Cast of Characters

The *Taking Off* Workbook features an engaging cast of characters enrolled in a beginning English class. The author developed the book around these characters to help students learn new language from familiar and engaging faces.

Jane Craft
American

Marco Diaz
Colombian

Luna Gilbert
Brazilian

Aziza Hassan
Somali

Thomas Jover
Haitian

Lin Kwok
Chinese

Eva Martinez
Colombian

Erik Mendez
Brazilian

Alex Reyes
Mexican

Ivan Stoli
Russian

Ly Tran
Vietnamese

David Vo
Vietnamese

Mei Wu
Chinese

Table of Contents

Table of Contents

Unit 1 Welcome to the classroom.

Workbook Lessons	Workbook Pages	Student Book Pages
Welcome!	2	3
The Alphabet: A–M	3	4
The Alphabet: N–Z	4	5–6
What's in the classroom?	5	7
Follow directions.	6	8–9
Close the book.	7	10–11
My phone number is (518) 555-7036.	8	12
Marco's Classroom	9	13
Grammar: *I'm, It's, What's*	10	14
Read and Write: An Emergency Form	11	15
Just for Fun	12	

A Complete.

| Jane | meet | Nice | David |

Jane: Hello. I'm ___Jane___.

David: Hi, Jane. I'm David. Nice to _____ you.

Jane: _____ to meet you too, _____.

B Complete.

| Alex | China | from | Hi | I'm |

Alex: ___Hi___. I'm _____. I'm _____ Mexico.

Mei: Hello. My name is Mei. _____ from _____.

C Write your name.

HELLO!

My name is

_____

A **Complete.**

A B C D E F G H I J K L M
A _____

a b c d e f g h i j k l m
a _____

B **Complete.**

A ____ C _____ F _____ I _____ L ____

a _____ d _____ g _____ k _____

C **Match.**

1. A   b
   B   e
   C   d
   D   g
   E   a
   F   f
   G   c

2. H   l
   I   k
   J   i
   K   h
   L   m
   M   j

A **Complete.**

N   O   P   Q   R   S   T   U   V   W   X   Y   Z

_N_ __ __ __ __ __ __ __ __ __ __ __ __

n   o   p   q   r   s   t   u   v   w   x   y   z

_n_ __ __ __ __ __ __ __ __ __ __ __ __

B **Complete.**

_N_ __ _P_ __ __ _S_ __ __ _V_ __ __ _Z_

_n_   o __ __ _r_ __ __ _u_ __ __ _x_ __ __

C **Complete.**

| first | How | last | spell | ~~What's~~ |

Eva: Hello. I'm Eva Martinez. _____ _What's_ _____ your name?

Ivan: My name is Ivan Stoli.

Eva: _____ do you

_____ that?

Ivan: My _____ name is I-V-A-N.

My _____ name is S-T-O-L-I.

A **Complete.**

backpack	board	book	chair
door	computer	student	paper
teacher	desk	notebook	pen

1. <u>backpack</u>

2. _____

3. _____

4. _____

What's your name?

5. _____

6. _____

★ Taking Off

7. _____

8. _____

9. _____

10. _____

11. _____

12. _____

A Circle.

book   backpack   notebook

B ✔ Check.

_____ pen   _____ paper   _____ board

C Complete.

My name is _____.

D Fill in.

Ⓐ pen   Ⓑ board   Ⓒ door

E Match.

1. _____ desk

a.

2. _____ paper

b.

Close the book.

A **Circle.**

1. Open the notebook.

2. Close the notebook.

3. Take out the book.

4. Go to the board.

B ✔ **Check.**

1. __✔__ Close the door.

_____ Point to the door.

_____ Close the book.

2. _____ Put away the book.

_____ Point to the paper.

_____ Put away the paper.

3. _____ Take out the pen.

_____ Take out the book.

_____ Take out the paper.

Welcome to the classroom. **7**

My phone number is (518) 555-7036.

A Complete.

eight	five	four	nine	~~one~~
seven	six	ten	three	two

1	2	3	4	5
one	_____	_____	_____	_____

6	7	8	9
_____	_____	_____	_____

B Write the numbers.

1. __1__ one
2. _____ seven
3. _____ two
4. _____ nine
5. _____ four
6. _____ five

C Complete.

address	email address	~~phone number~~

1. My _____ phone number _____ is (518) 555-7036.

2. My _____ is 234 Point Street.

3. My _____ is db107@freemail.com.

D Write about you.

1. My phone number is _____.

2. My address is _____.

3. My email address is _____.

A Read.

1 2 3 4 5 6 7 8 9 10
a b c d e f g h i j
k l m n o p q r s t
u v w x y z

Jane

Marco   Thomas   Ly

Marco's Classroom

    This is Marco's classroom. Jane is his teacher. Ly and Thomas are his classmates.

    Jane writes the alphabet on the board. She writes 10 numbers on the board. The students write the alphabet and the numbers on their papers.

B Look at the picture in Activity A. ✔ Check what you see.

I see ____.	Yes	No
ten numbers	✔	
the alphabet		
a door		
a board		
a book		

I see ____.	Yes	No
a computer		
a desk		
a student		
a teacher		
a paper		

A **Circle.**

1. (I'm) / What's Eva.

2. What's / It's a pencil.

3. I am / What is your name?

4. I'm / It's a notebook.

5. It's / What's this?

6. What is / I am Marco.

7. It is / What is a computer.

8. What is / I am from Mexico.

9. What is / I am this?

10. It is / I am a backpack.

B **Write 6 sentences.**

1. I'm _____ .

2. I'm _____ .

3. It's _____ .

4. It's _____ .

5. What's _____ ?

6. What's _____ ?

A Complete the form about you.

MCC MARINA Community College

Your Name: _____

       First Name   Last Name

IN AN EMERGENCY:

Please Call: _____

       First Name   Last Name

_____

Phone Number

B Write the names of 5 people in your family.

Example: _____ John Cruz _____

1. _____

2. _____

3. _____

4. _____

5. _____

A **Complete.**

~~board~~	book	chair	computer	desk
notebook	paper	pen	student	teacher

e	t	c	v	b	c	p	c	r	b	p	n	s
n	t	e	a	c	h	e	r	r	o	a	e	d
p	e	d	s	n	a	m	h	r	q	p	e	n
l	k	y	g	i	i	a	a	o	d	e	s	k
v	e	b	o	a	r	d	i	b	x	r	t	w
p	c	o	t	b	s	j	l	b	w	v	u	m
c	n	o	t	e	b	o	o	k	o	o	y	j
d	e	k	m	t	s	r	b	i	o	a	r	d
r	h	r	a	p	e	b	n	e	t	h	w	h
w	h	a	s	t	u	d	e	n	t	h	u	r
l	e	r	t	g	o	t	h	t	s	l	n	o
a	r	s	y	b	n	d	e	s	l	f	g	o
s	t	u	n	o	t	e	b	r	p	a	p	r

B **Go online!**

1. Go to a search engine. You can go to www.google.com or www.yahoo.com.

2. Type | ESL picture dictionary |.
   Click on [Search].

3. Find a dictionary you like.

4. Write the website address: _____

Unit 2 Where are you from?

Workbook Lessons	Workbook Pages	Student Book Pages
Where are you from?	14	19
What do you speak?	15	20
What does he speak?	16	21
She is married.	17	22
I am average height.	18	23–25
What's your address?	19	26
An Identification Form	20	27
Grammar: *Am, Is, Are, Has, Have*	21	28–29
Read: A Map	22	30
Write: My Classmate	23	31
Just for Fun	24	

A Look at the picture. Complete.

Alex: I'm from _____. Where are you from?

Mei: I'm from _____.

B Complete.

Alex   China   Mei   Mexico

Thomas: Where is _____ Alex _____ from?

Erik: He's from _____.

Thomas: Where is _____ from?

Erik: She's from _____.

C Write.

1. I'm from _____.

2. My teacher is from _____.

3. My classmate is from _____.

A Look at the picture. Complete.

Ivan: I speak _____. What do you speak?

David: I speak _____.

B Complete.

you	Spanish	~~speak~~	What

Mei: I _____ *speak* _____ Chinese.

_____ do _____

speak?

Marco: I speak _____.

C Write about you.

My name is _____.

I'm from _____.

I speak _____.

A Read.

Name	Country	Language
Alex	Mexico	Spanish
Aziza	Somalia	Somali
Luna	Brazil	Portuguese
Marco	Colombia	Spanish
Mei	China	Chinese

B Look at Activity A. Complete.

1. **A:** Marco is from _____Colombia_____. What does he speak?

   B: He speaks _____.

2. **A:** _____ is from Somalia. What does she speak?

   B: She speaks _____.

3. **A:** Luna is _____ Brazil. What does

   _____ speak?

   B: She _____ Portuguese.

4. **A:** _____ is from Mexico. What does he

   _____?

   B: He speaks _____.

5. **A:** Mei is from _____. What

   _____ she speak?

   B: She speaks _____.

Unit 2

She is married.

Student Book Page 22

A **Circle.**

1. (married)   single   divorced   widowed

2. married   single   divorced   widowed

3. married   single   divorced   widowed

B **Complete.**

| divorced | single | married | ~~widowed~~ |

1. <u>widowed</u>   2. _____   3. _____   4. _____

I am average height.

A **Complete.**

David   Alex   Lin   Mei

| average height | short | ~~tall~~ | tall |

1. Lin is _____ tall _____ .

2. David is _____ .

3. Alex is _____ .

4. Mei is _____ .

B **Complete.**

David   Alex   Mei

| don't have   has |

1. David _____ glasses.

2. Alex and Mei _____ glasses.

C **Write about you.**

I am _____ . I _____ glasses.

A **Complete.**

| eighteen | ~~eleven~~ | fifteen | fourteen | nineteen |
| seventeen | sixteen | thirteen | twelve | |

11	12	13	14	15
eleven	_____	_____	_____	_____

16	17	18	19
_____	_____	_____	_____

B **Write the numbers.**

1. __11__ eleven   2. _____ fourteen   3. _____ fifteen

4. _____ nineteen   5. _____ sixteen   6. _____ twelve

C **Complete.**

| address | My | ~~What's~~ | your | zip code |

Alex: _____ What's _____ your _____?

Lin: _____ address is 324 Short Street.

Alex: What's _____ zip code?

Lin: My _____ is 92924.

D **Write about you.**

My address is _____.

My zip code is _____.

An Identification Form

A Read about Luna.

Hi. My name is Luna J. Gilbert. I'm widowed. I have brown eyes. I have black hair. My address is 324 Green Street. My zip code is 12183. I live in Troy, New York.

B Complete the form for Luna.

IDENTIFICATION FORM

TYPE OR PRINT

Gilbert

LAST NAME	FIRST NAME	MI

ADDRESS	CITY	STATE	ZIP

CIRCLE ONE:

MARITAL STATUS:	SINGLE	MARRIED	DIVORCED	WIDOWED
EYE COLOR:	BLUE	BROWN	GREEN	BLACK
HAIR COLOR:	BROWN	BLACK	GRAY	RED	BLOND

A **Write *am*, *is*, or *are*.**

1. Mei _____ is _____ from China.

2. I _____ from Colombia.

3. Luna and Erik _____ from Brazil.

4. You _____ from Haiti.

5. Ivan _____ from Russia.

B **Write *has* or *have*.**

1. Luna _____ has _____ black hair.

2. You _____ blue eyes.

3. Thomas _____ brown hair.

4. I _____ gray hair.

5. They _____ blond hair.

C **Write *am*, *is*, *are*, *has*, or *have*.**

1. David _____ is _____ from Vietnam.

2. Alex and Anita _____ from Mexico.

3. Jane and Ivan _____ green eyes.

4. Mei _____ black hair.

5. Luna _____ brown eyes

6. We _____ from Vietnam.

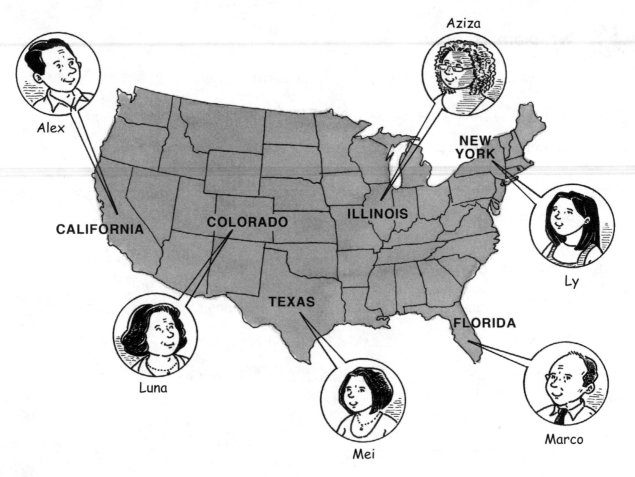

A Circle.

Where are the students?

1. Alex is in **Texas / Florida / California**.

2. Mei is in **New York / Texas / Illinois**.

3. Marco is in **California / Florida / Texas**.

4. Ly is in **New York / Florida / Colorado**.

5. Luna is in **Florida / Illinois / Colorado**.

6. Aziza is in **California / Texas / Illinois**.

A Write about a classmate.

1. My classmate's name is _____.

2. My classmate speaks _____.

3. My classmate is from _____.

4. My classmate is _____.
   (tall, average height, short)

5. My classmate has _____ eyes and _____ hair.

B Write about you.

1. My name is _____.

2. I speak _____.

3. I am from _____.

4. I am _____.
   (tall, average height, short)

5. I have _____ eyes and _____ hair.

C Write about your teacher.

1. My teacher's name is _____.

2. My teacher speaks _____.

3. My teacher is from _____.

4. My teacher is _____.
   (tall, average height, short)

5. My teacher has _____ eyes and _____ hair.

A **What are the words?**

Across →

2. Ivan is tall. Mei is short. I'm _____ height.

5. I'm from China. I speak _____.

Down ↓

1. Where are you _____?

2. My _____ is 23 Paper Street.

3. ten _____ twelve

4. My zip _____ is 92224.

B **Complete.**

1. I'm from Russia. I speak _____.

2. I'm from China. I speak _____.

3. I'm from Brazil. I speak _____.

4. I'm from Mexico. I speak _____.

C **Go online!**

1. Go to a search engine.

2. Type [(your country) flag]. Click on [Search].

3. Find a website with a picture of your country's flag.

4. Print the picture and bring it to class.

This is my family.

Workbook Lessons	Workbook Pages	Student Book Pages
Ly Tran's Family	26	35–36
Who is that?	27	37
Ivan's Relatives	28	38–39
Mr., Mrs., Ms., and *Miss*	29	40
Do you have children?	30	41
How old are you?	31	42
A Family Form	32	43
Grammar: *Do/Don't* and Pronouns	33	44–45
Read: David's Favorite Relative	34	46
Write: My Family	35	47
Just for Fun	36	

A Look at Ly's family tree. Complete.

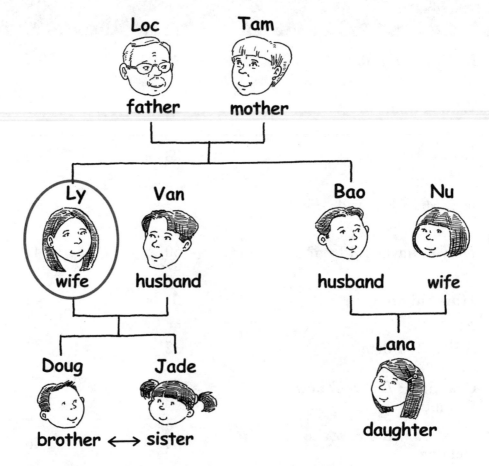

1. **Kim:** What's your husband's name?

   Ly: His name is ___Van___.

2. **Kim:** What's your mother's name?

   Ly: Her name is _____.

3. **Kim:** What's your father's name?

   Ly: His name is _____.

4. **Kim:** What's your brother's name?

   Ly: His name is _____.

B Look at the pictures in Activity A. Complete.

> ~~brother~~   wife   daughter   sister

1. Bao is Ly's ___brother___.

2. Lana is Nu's _____.

3. Jade is Doug's _____.

4. Nu is Bao's _____.

Unit 3 — Who is that?

A Look at the picture on page 26. Complete.

Loc

1. **A:** Who is that?

   B: Ly's _____ father _____.

Tam

2. **A:** Who is that?

   B: Ly's _____.

Doug

3. **A:** Who is that?

   B: Jade's _____.

B Look at the pictures on page 26. Fill in.

1. **Who is Loc?**

   Ⓐ Tam's brother.

   ● Tam's husband.

2. **Who is Doug?**

   Ⓐ Jade's brother.

   Ⓑ Jade's sister.

3. **Who is Lana?**

   Ⓐ Nu's daughter.

   Ⓑ Nu's son.

4. **Who is Ly?**

   Ⓐ Van's wife.

   Ⓑ Van's sister.

5. **Who is Nu?**

   Ⓐ Bao's wife.

   Ⓑ Bao's sister.

6. **Who is Tam?**

   Ⓐ Ly's father.

   Ⓑ Ly's mother.

This is my family. 27

A **Complete Ivan's family tree.**

Sophie is Ivan's mother. Yakov is Ivan's father. Yana is Yakov's sister. Pavel is Ivan's grandfather. Olga is Ivan's grandmother. Anton is Ivan's brother. Nelli is Anton's wife. Lara is Anton's daughter.

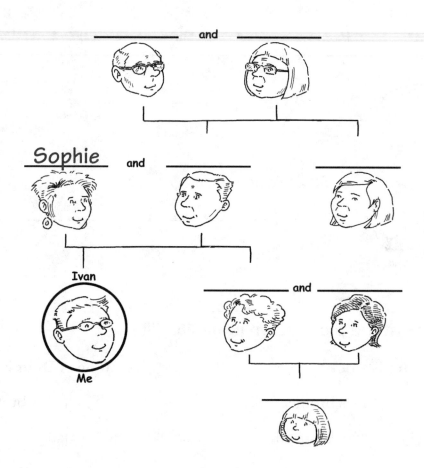

B **Write *middle-aged, old,* or *young.***

1. Anton's daughter is _____ young _____.

2. Ivan's grandfather is _____.

3. Ivan's father is _____.

C **Write about you.**

I am _____.

Mr., Mrs., Ms., and *Miss*

A   **Look at the family tree on page 28. Write *Mr., Mrs., Ms.,* or *Miss.***

Ivan

1. _____Mr._____ Stoli

Pavel   Olga

2. _____ and _____ or _____ Stoli

Lara

3. _____ or _____ Stoli

Yana

4. _____ or _____ Stoli

Nelli

5. _____ or _____ Stoli

Anton

6. _____ Stoli

Sophie

7. _____ or _____ Stoli

Do you have children?

A **Complete.**

| ~~children~~ daughter Do don't I No three |

David: Do you have _____ children _____?

Kim: No, I _____.

Ly: Yes, I have a son and a _____.

Alex: _____ you have children?

Jane: _____, I don't.

Luna: Yes, _____ have

_____ sons.

B **Write about you.**

Jane: Do you have children?

You: _____.

A **Write the numbers.**

1. ___90___ ninety
2. _____ twenty-two
3. _____ fifty
4. _____ seventy
5. _____ thirty
6. _____ forty
7. _____ one hundred
8. _____ fifty
9. _____ sixty
10. _____ eighty

B **Write the numbers.**

_20_   _30_   ___   ___   ___   ___   _80_   ___   _100_

C **Complete.**

| How | ~~old~~ | years | you | 68 |

Eva: How _____ old _____ are you?

Luna: I'm 52 _____ old.

_____ old are

_____?

Eva: I'm _____ years old.

D **Write about you.**

Jane: How old are you?

You: I'm _____.

A Family Form

A **Read about Alex's family.**

My name is Alex J. Reyes. I live with my parents, Juan M. Reyes and Anita S. Reyes. I also live with my wife, Linda F. Reyes, and my aunt, Ana T. Santos. I live with my son, Ben S. Reyes, and my daughter, Lola C. Reyes, too.

I am 48. Juan and Anita are 70. Linda is 46. Ana is 74. Lola is 17. Ben is 15.

Alex

B **Complete Alex's form.**

Census Form

Address: 178 Old Street

Troy	N.Y.	12183
City	State	Zip Code

List all the people at your address.

	First Name	MI	Last Name	Age
1.	Alex	J.	Reyes	48
2.				
3.				
4.				
5.				
6.				
7.				

A   **Look at Ly's family tree on page 26. Circle.**

1. **Thomas:** Do you have two children?
    Ly: ⟨Yes, I do.⟩ / No, I don't.

2. **Aziza:** Do you have two sons?
    Ly: Yes, I do. / No, I don't.

3. **Thomas:** Do you have a brother?
    Ly: Yes, I do. / No, I don't.

4. **Aziza:** Do you have a sister?
    Ly: Yes, I do. / No, I don't.

5. **Thomas:** Do you have a husband?
    Ly: Yes, I do. / No, I don't.

6. **Aziza:** Do you have a daughter?
    Ly: Yes, I do. / No, I don't.

B   **Complete.**

Her	Their	His	~~my~~	His

This is _____ my _____ mother. _____ name is Sophie. This is my father. _____ name is Yakov. I have a brother. _____ name is Anton. He has a wife and a daughter. _____ names are Nelli and Lara.

Ivan

C   **Write about you.**

1. **Jane:** Do you have a brother?
    You: _____.

2. **Jane:** Do you have a sister?
    You: _____.

A **Read.**

David's Favorite Relative

David's favorite relative is his brother. His brother's name is John. John is tall and young. He has brown eyes and black hair. John is from Vietnam. Now he lives in the United States. John lives with his wife Tina. He lives with his daughter Ruby, too.

David   John

B ✔ **Check.**

What is this story about?

_____ 1. John is David's favorite relative.

_____ 2. David is John's favorite relative.

C **Circle.**

1. John is **tall / short**.

2. John has **black / brown** hair.

3. John is from **the United States / Vietnam**.

4. John has **one daughter / one son**.

5. John is David's **uncle / brother**.

6. John has **black / brown** eyes.

7. John is **married / single**.

8. Ruby is John's **wife / daughter**.

Write: My Family

A Complete.

My Family

from live ~~name~~	My _____ name _____ is Marco Chavez. My family is _____ Colombia. I _____ in the United States now.
daughter children sons	I have four _____. I have one _____ and three _____.
Their people young	My children are _____. _____ names are Serena, Marco, Juan, and Miguel. I have five _____ in my family.
Their children Her sister She	I have one _____. _____ name is Clara. _____ lives in the United States, too. She has two _____. _____ names are Rosa and Pedro.

A Complete.

| daughter | ~~father~~ | mother | son |

1. Your mother's husband is your __f__ __a__ __t__ __h__ __e__ __r__
   8   5

2. Your girl child is your ____ ____ ____ ____ ____ ____ ____
   3   2   10   4

3. Your daughter's brother is your ____ ____ ____
   6

4. Your father's wife is your ____ ____ ____ ____ ____ ____
   7   1   9

B Write the letters from Activity A.

Y ____ ____ . ____ ____ __e__ ____ ____ __a__ ____ ____ !
   1   2   3   4   5   6   7   8   9   10

C Go online!

1. Go to www.maps.google.com. Type in your home address.

   | (your home address) | . Click | Search | .

2. Click on your address.

3. Click | Satellite | in the right corner of the map.

4. Print the picture and bring it to class.

Workbook Lessons	Workbook Pages	Student Book Pages
Ly's in the kitchen.	38	55
Is there a chair in the living room?	39	56
There's a stove in the kitchen.	40	57–58
I need a table.	41	59
Where do you cook?	42	60–61
18 or 80?	43	62
A Garage Sale	44	63
Grammar: Singular and Plural Nouns	45	64–65
Read: Mei's Apartment	46	66
Write: A Note	47	67
Just for Fun	48	

A Complete.

bathroom	bedroom	dining room
~~kitchen~~	living room	backyard

Lana and Ly

Doug

Jade

1. ___kitchen___ 2. _____ 3. _____

Loc

Van

Tam

4. _____ 5. _____ 6. _____

B Look at the pictures in Activity A. Complete.

1. Lana and Ly are in the ___kitchen___.

2. Loc is in the _____.

3. Jade is in the _____.

4. Van is in the _____.

5. Tam is in the _____.

A **Complete.**

| chair | kitchen | No | ~~there~~ | Yes |

Luna: Is ___there___ a _____ in the living room?

Erik: _____, there is.

Luna: Is there a lamp in the _____?

Erik: _____, there isn't.

B **Look at the picture. Circle.**

1. Is there a lamp in the living room?   (Yes, there is.)   No, there isn't.

2. Is there a chair in the living room?   Yes, there is.   No, there isn't.

3. Is there a bed in the bedroom?   Yes, there is.   No, there isn't.

4. Is there a table in the kitchen?   Yes, there is.   No, there isn't.

5. Is there a chair in the bathroom?   Yes, there is.   No, there isn't.

Welcome to our house. 39

A Circle.

1. There's a stove in the _____. bathroom (kitchen)
2. There's a closet in the _____. backyard bedroom
3. There's a microwave in the _____. kitchen backyard
4. There's a refrigerator in the _____. dining room kitchen
5. There's a sink in the _____. bathroom bedroom
6. There's a tub in the _____. kitchen bathroom

B Complete.

| ~~apartment~~ | house | rented room |

Mei   Alex   Luna

1. __apartment__   2. _____   3. _____

C Complete.

1. Luna lives in a ____rented room____.

2. Mei lives in an _____.

3. Alex lives in a _____.

D Write about you.

I live in _____.

A Read.

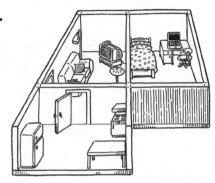

Mei's new apartment

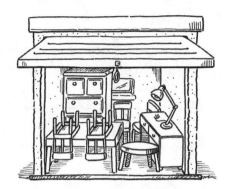

Eva's garage

Mei has a new apartment. She has some furniture. She needs more furniture. Eva has furniture for Mei. The furniture is in her garage.

B Complete.

desk	need	Thanks	~~What~~	you

Eva: _____What_____ do _____ need?

Mei: I _____ a bed.

Eva: Do you need a _____?

Mei: No, I don't. _____.

C Look at the picture in Activity A. Complete.

chairs	a desk	a dresser	~~lamps~~	a sofa	a table	a bed

Mei has:	Mei needs:
lamps	

Where do you cook?

Student Book Pages 60–61

A Complete.

bathroom	bedroom	living room	kitchen
cook	~~shower~~	sleep	study

1. **A:** Where do you _____ shower _____?

   B: I shower in the _____.

2. **A:** Where do you _____?

   B: I cook in the _____.

3. **A:** Where do you _____?

   B: I study in the _____.

4. **A:** Where do you _____?

   B: I sleep in the _____.

B Complete.

at the beach	in the city	in the country

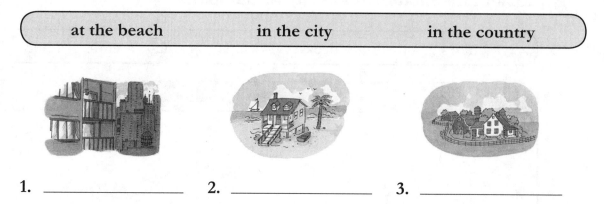

1. _____   2. _____   3. _____

A **Write the numbers.**

1. ___30___ thirty
2. _____ twelve
3. _____ thirteen
4. _____ twenty
5. _____ eighteen
6. _____ ninety
7. _____ eighty
8. _____ nineteen

B **Write the words for the numbers.**

1. 70 ___seventy___
2. 60 _____
3. 17 _____
4. 50 _____
5. 16 _____
6. 15 _____

C **Write the numbers.**

1. (twenty) There are ___20___ apartments.
2. (sixty) The house is _____ years old.
3. (eighteen) My address is _____ Pen Street.
4. (fourteen) There are _____ students in my class.
5. (twelve) There are _____ chairs in my house.
6. (fifty) I have _____ CDs.
7. (seventeen) My daughter is _____ years old.
8. (nineteen) I need _____ chairs.

A Match.

1. __e__ David needs a bike.

a.

2. _____ Ivan needs a lamp.

b.

3. _____ Aziza needs a fan.

c.

4. _____ Thomas needs a backpack.

d.

5. _____ Mei needs CDs.

e.

B Write 9 things in your house.

____sofa____   _____   _____

_____   _____   _____

_____   _____   _____

A Circle the plural nouns. Underline the singular nouns.

Aziza lives in a beach <u>house</u>. She likes beaches. She lives with her husband and their two daughters. Her house has three bedrooms, two bathrooms, a living room, a kitchen, a dining room, and five closets. Her house does not have a backyard.

There are two sofas in the living room. There are four chairs and a table in the dining room. There are four beds in Aziza's house. There are four dressers, too.

B Write singular or plural nouns.

1. a kitchen   two _____**kitchens**_____

2. a _____   four tubs

3. a house   five _____

4. a _____   three closets

5. a bathroom   two _____

6. a _____   eight chairs

C Write *a* or *an*.

David lives in ____**an**____ apartment in _____ city. His apartment has _____ bedroom, _____ bathroom, _____ kitchen, _____ living room, and _____ closet. It has _____ air conditioner, _____ stove, and _____ refrigerator.

A **Read.**

Mei lives in a city. She lives in an apartment building. Her apartment building has four floors. There are 14 apartments on a floor.

Mei lives in apartment 412. It has a bedroom, a living room, a bathroom, and a kitchen. Mei likes her kitchen. She cooks dinner in her kitchen every night. She eats in her kitchen. She studies in her kitchen, too.

B ✔ **Check.**

What is the story about?

_____ **1.** Mei's kitchen

_____ **2.** Mei's apartment

C ✔ **Check Yes or No.**

	Yes	No
1. Mei lives in the country.		✔
2. Mei lives in an apartment.		
3. Mei's apartment building has 4 floors.		
4. Mei's building has 14 apartments.		
5. Mei's apartment has two bedrooms.		
6. Mei studies in the living room.		
7. Mei's apartment has a dining room.		
8. Mei eats in the kitchen.		

A **Read.**

Mei lives in Mrs. Kim's apartment building. Mei's address is 456 White Street. She lives in apartment 412. Mei's phone number is (518) 555-2705. She has a problem in her apartment. She writes to Mrs. Kim.

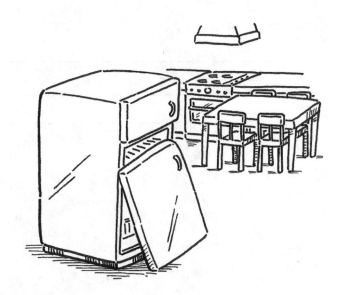

B **Complete Mei's note. Look at the picture in Activity A.**

412	~~Kim~~	refrigerator	(518) 555-2705
456	door	kitchen	

Dear Mrs. _____ Kim _____,

    I live at _____ White Street. I live in

apartment _____. I have a broken

_____ in the _____.

Please fix the _____. My phone number is

_____.

                 Thank you,

                 Mei Wong

A **Find the words.**

~~bed~~ chair desk dresser fireplace lamp rug sofa table

f	d	d	e	s	k	l	b	m	p
f	i	r	e	p	l	a	c	e	r
s	y	j	e	a	b	r	h	k	o
c	h	a	l	s	r	q	a	s	r
v	b	m	e	a	s	b	i	r	g
r	g	u	d	r	e	e	r	s	t
f	i	t	p	l	a	d	r	s	o
b	l	a	m	p	e	d	u	k	s
q	u	b	b	o	p	f	g	e	a
l	m	l	a	m	d	s	f	l	v
s	e	e	j	k	s	o	f	a	s
d	r	e	s	p	m	a	a	l	h

B

1. Find your dream house. Go to www.google.com.

2. Click <u>Images</u> in the top left corner.

3. Type [city house] or [beach house] or [country house].

4. Click [Search]. Pick your dream house. Print the picture and bring it to class.

Unit 5 — I talk on the phone.

Workbook Lessons	Workbook Pages	Student Book Pages
I listen to music every day.	50	71
Days and Months	51	72–73
Aziza gets up at 6:30.	52	74–75
Making an Appointment	53	76
How often do you study?	54	77
Ordinal Numbers	55	78
A Medical Form	56	79
Grammar: Simple Present Tense	57	80–81
Read: Marco's Birthday	58	82
Write: An Email	59	83
Just for Fun	60	

A Match.

1. __c__ I comb my hair.

   a.

2. _____ I listen to music.

   b.

3. _____ I read the newspaper.

   c.

4. _____ I work on my computer.

   d.

5. _____ I talk on the phone.

   e.

6. _____ I eat breakfast.

   f.

B Complete.

| do | day | brush | ~~What~~ |

David: ___What___ _____ you do every _____?

Eva: I _____ my teeth.

A **Complete the calendar.**

Friday	Monday	Thursday	
Tuesday	Wednesday	Saturday	~~Sunday~~

Marco's Week

Sunday	___	___	___	___	___	___
12	**13**	**14**	**15**	**16**	**17**	**18**
garage sales	English class	cook dinner	English class	work	go to brother's house for dinner	play soccer with Alex
study with Lin		study with Lin				

B **Look at the calendar in Activity A. Complete.**

1. Marco goes to garage sales on _____ Sunday _____ .

2. Marco goes to his brother's house on _____ .

3. Marco and Lin study on _____ and

   _____ .

4. Marco goes to English class on _____ and

   _____ .

C **Complete.**

~~August~~	December	February	January	March	October

1. Aug. = _____ August _____   2. Feb. = _____

3. Mar. = _____   4. Dec. = _____

5. Jan. = _____   6. Oct. = _____

I talk on the phone. 51

Aziza gets up at 6:30.

A **Match.**

1. __b__ 7:00   **a.** two fifteen

2. _____ 4:30   ~~**b.**~~ seven o'clock

3. _____ 2:15   **c.** four thirty

4. _____ 9:45   **d.** nine forty-five

B **Look at the pictures. Complete the sentences about Aziza's day.**

1. Aziza gets up at ___6:30___.   2. Aziza showers at _____.

3. Aziza eats breakfast at _____.   4. Aziza goes to class at _____.

C **Write about you.**

I get up at _____. I eat breakfast at _____. I go to class at

_____. I shower at _____.

A Complete.

| appointment | at | Can | fine | ~~like~~ | make |

Alex: I'd _____ like _____ to _____ an

_____ for a tune-up.

Man: _____ you come on Monday at 7:00?

Alex: Monday _____ 7:00? That's

_____.

B Look at the picture. Complete.

Eva: I'd like to make an appointment for a _____ haircut _____.

Woman: Can you come on _____ at 3:45?

Eva: _____ at 3:45? That's fine.

How often do you study?

Student Book Page 77

A Complete.

haircut	~~What~~	garage	once

Luna: _____**What**_____ do you do _____ a week?

Erik: I get a _____.

David: I go to _____ sales.

B Circle.

──────── Thomas's month ────────						
Sunday	Monday	Tuesday	Wednesday	Thursday	Friday	Saturday
study English	study English	study English	study English	study English	study English	study English shop for food
study English	study English get a haircut	study English	study English	study English	study English	study English shop for food
study English	study English	study English	study English	study English	study English	study English shop for food
study English	study English	study English	study English	study English	study English	study English shop for food

1. Thomas shops for food _____.   (once a week)   once a month

2. Thomas gets a haircut _____.   once a week   once a month

3. Thomas studies English _____.   every day   once a week

A Match.

1. __j__ 3rd   **a.** fourth
2. _____ 1st   **b.** second
3. _____ 5th   **c.** thirteenth
4. _____ 7th   **d.** eighth
5. _____ 2nd   **e.** fourteenth
6. _____ 8th   **f.** eighteenth
7. _____ 14th   **g.** first
8. _____ 13th   **h.** seventh
9. _____ 4th   **i.** fifth
10. _____ 18th   **j.** third

B Write the numbers.

1. ___9th___ ninth   2. _____ third
3. _____ eleventh   4. _____ seventh
5. _____ fourteenth   6. _____ eighth
7. _____ first   8. _____ sixth
9. _____ thirteenth   10. _____ ninth
11. _____ fifth   12. _____ twelfth

C Write about you.

My date of birth is the _____.

A Medical Form

A Complete the chart for Eva.

Hi. I'm Eva S. Martinez. I was born on September 6, 1939.

Hilltop Health Clinic (518) 555-4567

Medical History

Martinez			
Last Name	First Name	MI	Date of Birth

B Read. Answer the questions.

Hilltop Health Clinic (518) 555-4567

Medical History

Jover	Thomas	H.	8/26/81
Last Name	First Name	MI	Date of Birth

1. What is Thomas's last name? _____

2. What is Thomas's middle initial? _____

3. What is Thomas's date of birth? _____

Unit 5

Grammar: Simple Present Tense

Student Book
Pages
80–81

A **Complete. Add -s when necessary.**

1. **(eat)** I _____ breakfast every day.

2. **(cook)** Marco _____ on Mondays.

3. **(play)** David _____ soccer on Saturdays.

4. **(work)** Linda and Alex _____ every day.

5. **(need)** My brother _____ a bike.

6. **(shop)** Aziza _____ for food once a week.

7. **(get)** Jane _____ a haircut once a month.

8. **(study)** My husband and I _____ English every day.

9. **(sleep)** I _____ in the bedroom.

10. **(talk)** Ly _____ on the phone every day.

B **Write *am*, *is*, or *are*.**

1. **Ly:** Hi, Mei. How are you today?

   Mei: I ____*am*____ fine.

2. **Thomas:** It _____ my birthday today!

   Aziza: Happy Birthday, Thomas!

3. **Alex:** Where is Eva?

   Luna: Eva and Jane _____ in the backyard.

4. **Marco:** What time is it?

   Eva: It _____ 7:45. We _____ in class.

A **Read.**

Today is June 17. It is Marco's birthday. Marco is 42 years old. Marco goes to class at 3:00. Class starts at 3:15. There is a party in class. Luna brings a cake. David brings CDs. Aziza takes photos of the students and the teacher. Marco opens presents. He eats cake. He talks with his classmates. He is happy.

B **Circle.**

1. (It's June 17.)   It's June 24.

2. Marco is 42.   Marco is 24.

3. The party is at Marco's house.   The party is in class.

4. Class is at 3:00.   Class is at 3:15.

5. Erik brings a cake.   Luna brings a cake.

6. David brings CDs.   David brings photos.

7. Aziza takes photos.   The teacher takes photos.

8. The teacher is at the party.   The teacher is not at the party.

A **Complete.**

| nice | movies | once | ~~photos~~ | study | go | month |

☑ Marco

Marco

Dear Juan,

These are _____ *photos* _____ of my

classmates. They are very _____.

Mei and I _____ to garage sales

_____ a week. David is from Vietnam.

David and I go to the _____ once a

_____. Aziza is from Somalia. Aziza and I

_____ on Saturdays.

Love, Marco

B **Write an email about 3 classmates.**

Dear _____,

_____

_____

_____

_____

A **Complete.**

J a n u a r y
      6

F _ _ _ _ _ _ _
  10

M a r c h
    1

A p r i l
13   4

M _ _

_ _ _ _
8 3

_ _ _ _ _

A _ _ _ _
    5 11

S e p t e m b e r

O _ _ _ _ _
    7   9

N o v e m b e r

D e c e m b e r
12   2

B **Write the letters from Activity A. Answer the question.**

W _ _ _ _ _ _ _ _ _
  1 2 3   4 5   6 7 8 9

_ _ _ _ _ _ _ _?
10 4 9 11 1 12 13 6

It's in _____.

C Go online!

1. Find a place to get a haircut in your town. Go to a search engine.

2. Type | haircut (your zip code) |.
   Click on | Search |.

3. Write down the phone numbers and addresses of three places.

Workbook Lessons	Workbook Pages	Student Book Pages
I'm looking for shoes.	62	87–88
What are you wearing to the party?	63	89–90
What's your favorite color?	64	91
What size are you?	65	92
The pants are too short.	66	93
Money	67	94
Writing a Check	68	95
Grammar: Adjectives and Nouns	69	96–97
Read: A Catalog	70	98
Write: Ly's Shopping List	71	99
Just for Fun	72	

A Complete.

a coat	a dress	pants	a skirt
~~shoes~~	a suit	a sweater	a watch

1. __shoes__   2. _____   3. _____   4. _____

5. _____   6. _____   7. _____   8. _____

B Complete.

~~Excuse~~	looking	me	Thank	watch

Luna: ____Excuse____ me. I'm _____ for

a _____.

Clerk: Follow _____, please.

Luna: _____ you.

C Complete.

help	I	jacket	~~May~~

Clerk: ____May____ I _____ you?

Alex: Yes, _____ need a _____.

A **Complete.**

| and | are | dress | I'm | ~~What~~ | wearing |

Kim: _____What_____ are you _____ to the party?

David: _____ wearing black pants _____ a blue shirt.

What _____ you wearing?

Kim: I'm wearing a purple _____.

B **Circle.**

clerk   Linda   Alex   Lola   Anita   Juan

1. Alex is wearing _____.   a suit   (pants and a shirt)

2. Linda is wearing _____.   pants   a sweater

3. Lola is wearing _____.   pants   a skirt

4. Anita is wearing _____.   a blouse   a skirt

5. Juan is wearing _____.   a shirt   a sweater

6. The clerk is wearing _____. a suit   a dress

A Complete.

| blue | color | favorite | My | ~~What~~ |

Thomas: _____What_____ is your _____ color?

Marco: _____ favorite _____ is

_____.

B Complete.

| Brown | color | dress | ~~is~~ | your |

Ivan: What color _____is_____ your _____?

Aziza: Red.

Ivan: What _____ are _____ shoes?

Aziza: _____.

C Write about you.

Jane: What are you wearing?

You: I'm wearing _____.

Jane: What color are your shoes?

You: _____.

Jane: What color is your shirt?

You: _____.

Jane: What color are your pants?

You: _____.

A Write *small*, *medium*, or *large*.

1. __medium__   2. _____   3. _____

B Complete.

| you | I'm | What | ~~size~~ | medium | are |

Mei: What _____ size _____ are

_____?

Alex: I'm a _____.

_____ size

_____ you?

Mei: _____ a small.

C Write about you.

Jane: What size are you?

You: I'm a _____.

A Complete.

Alex   Eva   Ivan   Mei

| too big   too long   too small   too long   too big   too short |

1. Alex's pants are _____ too long _____.

2. Ivan's pants are _____.

3. Eva's shoes are _____.

4. Eva's hat is _____.

5. Mei's shoes are _____.

6. Mei's coat is _____.

B Write sentences about Thomas's clothes.

1. Thomas's pants are too short _____.

2. _____.

3. _____.

Thomas

A Complete.

| 25¢ | ~~1 cent~~ | 10 cents | a nickel | a quarter |

1. a penny

    __1 cent__

    1¢

2. _____

    5 cents

    5¢

3. a dime

    _____

    10¢

4. _____

    25 cents

    _____

B Write how much.

1. $25.25

2. _____

3.  _____

4. _____

A Read.

It is February 14, 2010. Ivan is at Clark's Department Store. He is buying pants. The pants are $37.80. He is paying by check.

Ivan Stoli
174 Maple Street
Riverton, NY 14246

DATE February 14, 2010   2-5654-1234

1179

PAY TO THE ORDER OF ___Clark's Department Store___ $ 37.80

Thirty-seven and 80/100 _____ DOLLARS

Lakeland
City Bank

MEMO ___pants___   *Ivan Stoli*

⑈012345⑈ ⑆123456543⑆01234567⑈

B Write a check.

It is December 20, 2010. You are at Sanford's Department Store. You are buying a sweater. The sweater is $26.05.

1179

DATE_____   2-5654-1234

PAY TO THE ORDER OF _____ $ _____

_____ DOLLARS

Lakeland
City Bank

MEMO _____

⑈012345⑈ ⑆123456543⑆01234567⑈

A **Look at the picture. Complete.**

Aziza   Alex   Lin   Erik   Mei

| short | skirt | ~~large~~ | pants | large | scarf |

1. Erik is wearing a _____ large _____ sweater.

2. Aziza is wearing a long _____.

3. Lin is wearing a _____ dress.

4. Erik is wearing short _____.

5. Alex is wearing a long _____.

6. Mei is wearing a _____ hat.

B **Write new sentences about the picture in Activity A.**

1. _____.

2. _____.

3. _____.

4. _____.

A Read.

A. CHILDREN'S JACKETS

Sizes: small, medium, large

Colors: red, yellow, green, or blue

Price: $22.50

B. MEN'S COATS

Sizes: small, medium, large, extra large

Colors: black, brown, or blue

Price: $88.99

C. WOMEN'S DRESSES

Sizes: small, medium, large

Colors: white, black, red, or pink

Price: $34.55

B Look at Activity A. Write the answers.

1. How much are the women's dresses? _____

2. What sizes are the children's jackets? _____

3. What colors are the men's coats? _____

4. How much are the children's jackets? _____

5. What colors are the women's dresses? _____

6. How much are the men's coats? _____

A Complete Ly's shopping list.

Price: $17.95   Price: $22.50   Price: $14.75   Price: $19.55   Price $18.25

1. **Jade:** A blue _____jacket_____   Size small $22.50

2. **Doug:** Brown pants   Size medium $ _____

3. **Loc:** A black _____   Size medium $19.55

4. **Van:** A yellow shirt   Size medium $ _____

5. **Tam:** A purple _____   Size small $18.25

B Write about you. Write a shopping list for your family.

	Name	Clothes	Size
1.			
2.			
3.			
4.			
5.			
6.			

A   **Circle the words.**

bathing suit	belt	blouse	cap	coat	dress
jacket	pants	scarf	shirt	shoes	skirt
socks	~~suit~~	sweater	watch		

a	s	b	a	t	h	i	n	b	e	l	t	m	s
s	c	a	r	f	r	m	a	t	l	c	a	n	w
o	t	t	c	n	p	s	o	a	h	o	r	l	e
c	y	h	d	a	w	a	t	c	h	s	u	e	a
k	a	i	r	a	p	k	n	n	v	w	s	s	e
s	c	n	e	o	p	s	k	t	a	e	k	k	e
b	k	g	s	h	o	e	s	t	s	a	i	i	t
m	l	s	s	w	e	a	u	x	h	t	b	r	a
j	a	u	k	e	t	c	i	t	i	e	c	t	i
a	t	i	s	c	o	a	t	m	r	r	u	q	f
c	b	t	a	b	l	o	s	f	t	s	u	t	g
k	r	z	f	j	a	c	k	e	t	p	a	n	i

B   **Go online!**

1. Find black pants. Go to a search engine. Type the name of your favorite department store. Click on [Search]. Click on the store's name. Find the search box.

2. Type [black pants].
   Click on [Search].

3. Write the price of a pair of pants you like. $ _____

I'm so hungry!

Workbook Lessons	Workbook Pages	Student Book Pages
We need some apples.	74	107
I'm looking for milk.	75	108–109
Breakfast, Lunch, and Dinner	76	110–111
A sandwich, please.	77	112
Do you have hamburgers for dinner?	78	113
Containers	79	114
A Potluck Dinner	80	115
Grammar: Count and Non-count Nouns	81	116–117
Read: Supermarket Coupons	82	118
Write: A Shopping List	83	119
Just for Fun	84	

A **Complete.**

| apples | ~~carrots~~ | eggs | ice cream | milk | potatoes |

  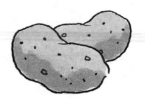

1. ___carrots___   2. _____   3. _____

4. _____   5. _____   6. _____

B **Complete.**

| some | ~~need~~ | right | potatoes | That's |

Alex: We _____ need _____ some apples.

Linda: That's _____. We need

_____ milk, too.

Alex: We need some _____.

Linda: _____ right.

A **Match.**

1. __e__ beef

2. _____ bread

3. _____ butter

4. _____ cake

5. _____ cheese

6. _____ chicken

7. _____ apples

a.

b.

c.

d.

e.

f.

g.

B **Complete.**

aisle   pasta   in   looking   ~~me~~

Ivan: Excuse ____me____. I'm looking for some lettuce.

Clerk: Lettuce is _____ aisle 1.

Ivan: I'm _____ for _____, too.

Clerk: Pasta is in _____ 5.

Breakfast, Lunch, and Dinner

A Complete.

> ~~breakfast~~   cereal   do   eggs   have   fish   sandwich

Aziza: What do you have for _____ **breakfast** _____?

Eva: I usually have _____.

I sometimes have _____.

Aziza: What _____ you have for lunch?

Eva: I always have a _____.

Aziza: What do you _____ for dinner?

Eva: I usually have _____. I sometimes have chicken.

B Match.

1. __b__ It's 12:00 P.M.   **a.** Let's have dinner.

2. _____ It's 6:00 P.M.   ~~**b.**~~ Let's have lunch.

3. _____ It's 8:00 A.M.   **c.** Let's have breakfast.

C Write about you.

I have breakfast at _____. I usually have

_____ for breakfast. I have lunch at _____.

I usually have _____ for lunch. Sometimes I have

_____. I have dinner at _____. I usually have

_____ for dinner.

A Complete.

pie	coffee	hamburger
~~pizza~~	soda	sandwich

1. ___pizza___ 2. _____ 3. _____

4. _____ 5. _____ 6. _____

B Complete.

drink	hamburger	~~May~~	thanks	soda

Server: _____May_____ I help you?

David: Yes. A _____, please.

Server: Anything to _____ today?

David: Yes, _____. Some

_____, please.

C Write about you.

Server: May I help you?

You: Yes. _____.

Do you have hamburgers for dinner?

A **Complete.**

| do | don't | for | have | ~~you~~ |

Ivan: Do ___you___ have hamburgers for dinner?

Thomas: No, I _____.

Ivan: Do you _____ pizza _____ dinner?

Thomas: Yes, I _____.

B **Look at the picture. Complete.**

| breakfast | chicken | ~~eggs~~ | lunch |

Thomas: Do you have ___eggs___ for _____?

Ivan: Yes, I do. Do you have _____ for _____?

Thomas: Yes, I do.

A Complete.

| bag | ~~bottle~~ | box | can | carton | jar |

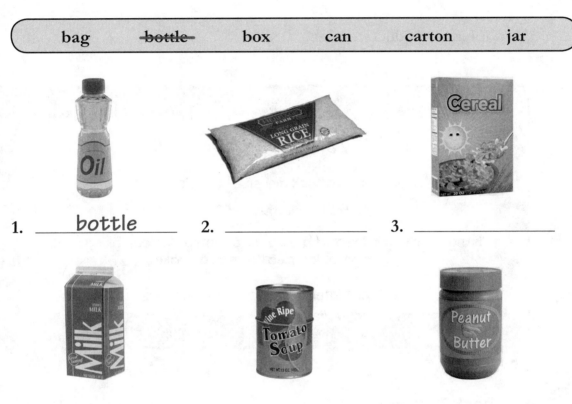

1. ___bottle___   2. _____   3. _____

4. _____   5. _____   6. _____

B Look at the pictures in Activity A. Complete.

| bag | ~~bottle~~ | box | jar | can | carton |

1. a ___bottle___ of oil

2. a _____ of milk

3. a _____ of peanut butter

4. a _____ of tomato soup

5. a _____ of rice

6. a _____ of cereal

A **Read.**

Luna is having a potluck dinner.

It's a party!

Come to a potluck dinner at Luna's house!

Friday night at 6:00.

Bring your favorite food from your country. You can bring fruit, vegetables, meat, drinks, or cake.

Let's eat interesting food and have fun!

B ✔ **Check *True* or *False*.**

	True	False
1. The potluck is at Luna's house.	✔	
2. A potluck is a party.		
3. Luna makes all the food.		
4. Many people bring food.		
6. The party is in the morning.		

C **Write about you.**

Jane: What is your favorite food?

You: My favorite food is _____.

A Read and ✔ check.

	Count	Non-count
1. I usually eat **pasta** for dinner.		✔
2. **Cake** is my favorite dessert.		
3. Alex eats **carrots** for lunch.		
4. I'm looking for **bread**.		
5. I need some **bananas**.		
6. A chicken **sandwich**, please.		
7. Luna likes **rice** for dinner.		
8. Mei and Aziza eat **cereal** for breakfast.		
9. I always have **lettuce** on my sandwiches.		
10. **Oranges** are David's favorite fruit.		

B Write the food words from Activity A in the correct box.

Count Nouns	Non-count Nouns
bananas	pasta

A Read.

B Write.

Eggs	Coffee	Rice
Price: __$3.75__	Price: __$9.50__	Price: __$7.10__
Coupon: __50¢__	Coupon: _____	Coupon: _____
Cost: _____	Cost: _____	Cost: _____

C Complete.

1. You have $10.00 and no coupons. A carton of milk is $2.30. You can buy _____ cartons of milk.

2. You have $14.00 and no coupons. You can buy _____ bag of rice.

3. You have $20.00 and no coupons. What can you buy? _____

    _____

A Look at Alex's shopping cart. Write a shopping list for Alex.

Shopping List

carrots

A Circle the words.

apples bananas beans beef bread butter cake
carrots cheese chicken eggs fish ice cream
lettuce milk oranges pasta potatoes rice

b	a	n	a	n	a	s	c	a	m	r	r	a	b
e	p	b	f	i	s	n	g	o	i	b	o	k	p
e	p	e	b	r	e	a	d	i	l	b	r	x	u
f	e	a	u	a	i	t	q	u	k	r	a	l	f
p	l	n	t	d	a	c	f	i	s	h	n	l	p
o	s	s	t	i	v	s	e	l	e	t	g	n	o
c	c	b	e	c	p	a	s	p	i	m	e	l	t
h	r	h	r	a	p	p	l	e	s	k	s	y	a
i	b	c	e	k	i	c	e	c	r	e	a	m	t
c	d	r	e	e	g	g	s	m	u	s	w	p	o
k	r	f	i	l	s	o	l	e	t	t	u	c	e
e	p	a	s	t	a	e	l	i	n	p	x	r	s
n	c	a	r	r	o	t	s	r	i	e	c	v	a

B Go online!

1. Think of your favorite lunch.

2. Go to www.google.com. Find a picture of each food.

3. Click on <u>Images</u> in the top left corner. Type in the food words.
   Click [Search].

4. Print a picture of each food and bring the pictures to class.

How's the weather?

Workbook Lessons	Workbook Pages	Student Book Pages
It's snowing.	86	123–124
What season do you like?	87	125
I'm playing soccer.	88	126–127
What do you like doing in the summer?	89	128
It's cold and windy.	90	129
What's the temperature?	91	130
A Weather Map	92	131
Grammar: Present Continuous Tense and Contractions	93	132–133
Read: Erik's Email	94	134
Write: Mei's Letter	95	135
Just for Fun	96	

A **Complete.**

cold	hot	raining	snowing	~~sunny~~	windy

1. ___sunny___

2. _____

3. _____

4. _____

5. _____

6. _____

B **Complete.**

cold	It's	Los Angeles	~~weather~~

Luna: How's the _____weather_____ in New York?

Alex: It's _____. How's the weather in

_____?

Luna: _____ hot.

A Write the seasons.

| winter | spring | ~~summer~~ | fall |

1. It's _____ summer _____.

2. It's _____.

3. It's _____.

4. It's _____.

B Complete.

| **What** | **like** | **Spring** | **don't** | ~~season~~ |

Eva: What ___season___ do you _____?

Ly: Fall.

Eva: _____ season _____ you like?

Ly: _____.

A Complete.

| watching TV | cooking | reading | dancing | walking | ~~playing soccer~~ |

1. <u>playing soccer</u>   2. _____   3. _____

4. _____   5. _____   6. _____

B Complete.

Alex and Linda   Ly   Erik   David

1. What are Linda and Alex doing? They're _____ dancing _____.

2. What's Ly doing? She's _____.

3. What is Erik doing? He's _____.

4. What's David doing? He's _____.

What do you like doing in the summer?

A **Complete.**

| do | doing | like | summer |

Mei: What _____do_____ you like _____ in the _____?

Ivan: I _____ swimming.

B **Look at the pictures. Complete.**

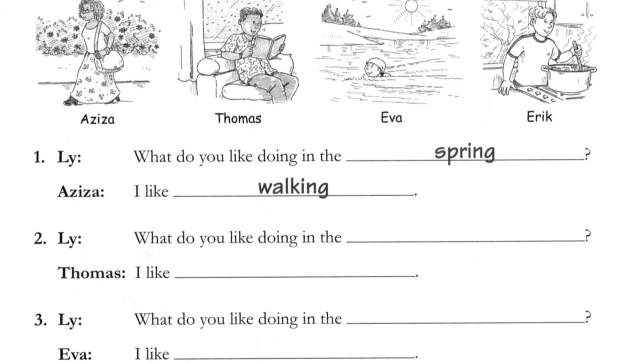

Aziza   Thomas   Eva   Erik

1. **Ly:** What do you like doing in the _____spring_____?

   Aziza: I like _____walking_____.

2. **Ly:** What do you like doing in the _____?

   Thomas: I like _____.

3. **Ly:** What do you like doing in the _____?

   Eva: I like _____.

4. **Ly:** What do you like doing in the _____?

   Erik: I like _____.

C **Write about you.**

Jane: What do you like doing in the summer?

You: _____.

A **Write about the weather.**

| cloudy | ~~cold~~ | cool | hot | raining | ~~snowing~~ | sunny | windy |

1. It's _____ cold _____.

   It's _____ snowing _____.

2. It's _____ and

   _____ .

3. It's _____ and

   _____ .

4. It's _____ and

   _____ .

A **Complete.**

| ~~30°/–1°~~ | 50°/10° | 70°/21° | 103°/39° |

1. It's cold.

    It's _____30°_____ F. It's _____–1°_____ C.

2. It's very hot!

    It's _____ F. It's _____ C.

3. It's warm today.

    It's _____ F. It's _____ C.

4. It's cool today.

    It's _____ F. It's _____ C.

A Read.

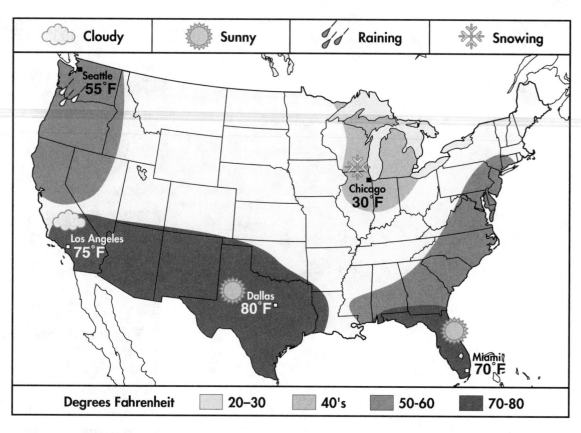

	Cloudy		Sunny		Raining		Snowing

Seattle
55°F

Chicago
30°F

Los Angeles
75°F

Dallas
80°F

Miami
70°F

Degrees Fahrenheit ▢ 20–30 ▢ 40's ▢ 50-60 ▢ 70-80

B Complete the chart.

City	Temp.*	Sunny	Raining	Snowing	Cloudy
Seattle	55° F		✔		
Los Angeles					
Dallas					
Chicago					
Miami					

*Temp. = Temperature

Grammar: Present Continuous Tense and Contractions

A **Complete.**

1. I _am_ eat_ing_ .

2. He _____ talk_____ .

3. We _____ read_____ .

4. They _____ sing_____ .

5. She _____ listen_____ .

6. You _____ study_____ .

B **Write sentences.**

1. Aziza/study/in the kitchen _Aziza is studying in the kitchen_ .

2. David and Thomas/play/soccer _____ .

3. Eva/buy/milk _____ .

4. Alex/cook/dinner _____ .

5. Ly and Van/eat/dinner _____ .

C **Write sentences. Use contractions.**

1. I/watch/TV _I'm watching TV_ .

2. We/buy/food _____ .

3. He/read/the newspaper _____ .

4. They/play/basketball _____ .

5. You/walk/home _____ .

D **Write about you.**

Jane: What are you doing?

You: _____

A Read.

Mei,

How are you? We are fine. We like Chicago. It's raining. It's cool and windy. We're having coffee in a café. David is listening to music. Eva is reading a book. Lin is watching the rain.

See you next week, Erik

B Complete. Add *-ing*.

| read | listen | watch | ~~drink~~ | rain | eat |

1. Erik and his friends are _____ drinking _____ coffee.

2. It's cool and it's _____.

3. Eva is _____ a book and

   _____ a sandwich.

4. David is _____ to music.

5. Lin is _____ the rain.

A **Look at the picture. You are Mei. Complete the letter.**

lunch	sister	in	hot	~~Dear~~	weather	talking

_____Dear_____ Erik,

I'm _____ San Diego. My

_____ is here, too. The _____

here is sunny and very _____. Today we are

_____ and having _____ in

the park.

Your friend,

Mei

A **What are the words?**

Across →

1. How's the _____?

4. It's 70° F. It's _____. The sun feels good.

5. It's cold and white outside. It's _____!

Down ↓

1. Oh no! My hat! It's so _____!

2. It's 101° F/38° C. It's _____.

3. It's cold and it's _____. I need an umbrella.

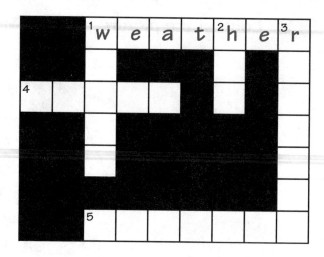

B **Go online!**

1. Find the weather in your town for three days. Go to www.google.com.

2. Type | weather (your city) |.
   Click on [Search].

3. Complete the chart.

City					
Day	**Temp.***	**Sunny**	**Raining**	**Snowing**	**Cloudy**

*Temp. = Temperature

Workbook Lessons	Workbook Pages	Student Book Pages
Places in Town	98	139
A Neighborhood Map	99	140
More Places in Town	100	141
Where's the laundromat?	101	142–143
Do you live near a post office?	102	144–145
Banking	103	146
Using an ATM	104	147
Grammar: Prepositions of Place	105	148–149
Read: Depositing a Check	106	150
Write: Lin's Application	107	151
Just for Fun	108	

A Complete.

bank	fire station	gas station
hospital	~~library~~	police station

1. _____library_____   2. _____   3. _____

4. _____   5. _____   6. _____

B Complete.

bank	going	there	I'm	about	together	~~Where~~

Thomas: _____Where_____ are you _____?

Erik: _____ going to the _____. What

_____ **you?**

Thomas: I'm going _____, too. Let's go

_____.

A **Complete.**

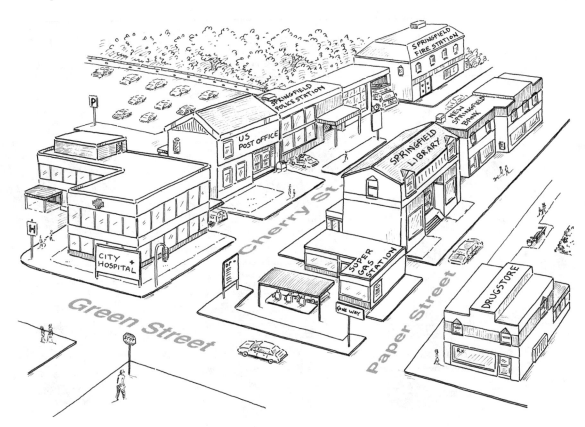

1. **Eva:** Excuse me. Where's the _____post office_____?

   Thomas: It's on Cherry Street.

   Eva: On _____? Thanks.

2. **Ivan:** Excuse me. Where's the _____?

   Mei: It's on Paper Street.

   Ivan: On _____? Thanks.

3. **Lin:** Excuse me. Where's the _____?

   Marco: It's on Cherry Street.

   Lin: On _____? Thanks.

More Places in Town

A Complete.

bus stop	laundromat	movie theater
park	~~restaurant~~	supermarket

1. __restaurant__

2. _____

3. _____

4. _____

5. _____

6. _____

B Complete.

| isn't | library | neighborhood | ~~there~~ |

Ly: Is ____there____ a restaurant in your neighborhood?

David: Yes, there is.

Ly: Is there a _____ in your _____?

David: No, there _____.

A Complete.

| between | on | next to | ~~drugstore~~ | Street | restaurant |

Aziza: Where's the _____ drugstore _____?

Ly: It's _____ State Street.

Aziza: On State _____?

Ly: That's right. It's _____ the post office and

the _____.

Aziza: Where's the laundromat?

Ly: It's _____ the bank.

B Look at the picture in Activity A. Write *between*, *next to*, and *on*.

1. The bank is _____ between _____ the laundromat and the

movie theater.

2. The movie theater is _____ the restaurant.

3. The laundromat is _____ 1st Street.

A **Complete.**

| do | don't | ~~live~~ | far from | you |

Eva: Do you _____live_____ near a post office?

Aziza: Yes, I _____.

Eva: Do _____ live _____ a bank?

Aziza: No, I _____.

B **Match.**

1. __b__ Where do you buy stamps?   a. At a laundromat.

2. _____ Where do you watch a movie?   ~~b.~~ At a post office.

3. _____ Where do you wash clothes?   c. At a bank.

4. _____ Where do you make a deposit?   d. At a movie theater.

C **Write about you.**

1. **Jane:** Do you live near a market?

   You: _____.

2. **Jane:** Do you live far from a restaurant?

   You: _____.

3. **Jane:** Where do you buy stamps?

   You: _____.

4. **Jane:** Where do you make a deposit?

   You: _____.

A Read.

Eva puts money in the bank every month. She is depositing three checks into her savings account. This is her deposit slip.

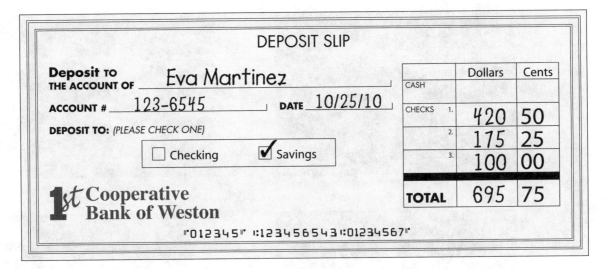

DEPOSIT SLIP

Deposit TO
THE ACCOUNT OF _____ Eva Martinez _____

ACCOUNT # _____ 123-6545 _____ DATE _____ 10/25/10 _____

DEPOSIT TO: *(PLEASE CHECK ONE)*

☐ Checking   ☑ Savings

1st Cooperative Bank of Weston

"012345" ":123456543":01234567"

	Dollars	Cents
CASH		
CHECKS 1.	420	50
2.	175	25
3.	100	00
TOTAL	695	75

B Complete.

1. The date is _____ October 25, 2010 _____.

2. Eva's account number is _____.

3. She is depositing a total of $_____.

4. She is depositing money into her _____ account.

5. She is depositing _____ checks.

A Read.

David is using an ATM. He is taking money from his checking account. He's making a withdrawal.

1.

2. Enter PIN / xxxx

3. Withdrawal
Deposit
Check balance

4.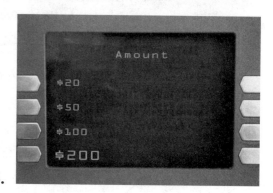
Amount
$20
$50
$100
$200

B Look at the pictures in Activity A. Circle.

1. David's PIN is 1256. He presses _____.   1-2-7-8   (1-2-5-6)

2. He is making a _____.   deposit   withdrawal

3. He is taking money from _____.   savings   checking

4. He is taking _____. $200.00 $40.00

A Write *in* or *on*.

1. Thomas is _____ **in** _____ the laundromat.

2. The laundromat is _____ Beach Street.

3. Thomas's jacket is _____ the chair.

4. Thomas's clothes are _____ the table.

5. Thomas's backpack is _____ the sofa.

6. Thomas's book is _____ his backpack.

B Write *next to*, *between*, or *across from*.

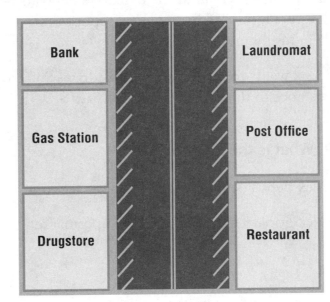

1. The restaurant is _____ **next to** _____ the post office.

2. The gas station is _____ the bank and the drugstore.

3. The laundromat is _____ the post office.

4. The drugstore is _____ the restaurant.

5. The post office is _____ the laundromat and the restaurant.

A **Read.**

Depositing a Check

Alex gets his paycheck on Monday. His check is $472.38. He has a checking account and a savings account at the bank. He deposits $447.38 in his checking account. Alex puts money in his savings account every week. This week, he deposits $25 in his savings account.

Today Alex wants to buy food. He withdraws $30 from his checking account. Alex goes to the supermarket. He pays $29.35. Now he has 65¢.

B ✔ **Check. What is the story about?**

_____ 1. Alex deposits money in his savings account.

_____ 2. Alex goes to the bank and the supermarket.

C **Complete.**

1. Alex's paycheck is $__472.38__.

2. Alex deposits $_____ in his checking account.

3. Alex deposits $_____ in his savings account.

4. Alex puts money in his savings account every _____.

5. Alex withdraws $30 to buy _____.

6. Now Alex has $_____ in his hand.

A Read.

NEW YORK STATE
Driver's License Number N89423

Lin Kwok

2484 Green Street, Apt 8
Troy, NY 12183
D.O.B.: 04-19-1966
Hair: black
Eyes: brown

B Fill in the form for Lin.

SUNNY SUPERMARKET   **Card Club Application**

Last Name	First Name	Home Phone

Street Address   Apartment #

City   State   Zip Code   Date of Birth
                                                       (month/day/year)

Driver's License Number   ► _____   _____
or State I.D. Number   Applicant's Signature   Date

Unit
9

Just for Fun

A **Complete.**

1. Where do you watch a movie?

   At a <u>m</u> <u>o</u> <u>v</u> <u>i</u> <u>e</u> <u>t</u> <u>h</u> <u>e</u> <u>a</u> <u>t</u> <u>e</u> <u>r</u>
   8 9   1   10

2. Where do you wash your clothes?

   At a ___ ___ ___ ___ ___ ___ ___ ___ ___
     2   5

3. Where do you buy aspirin?

   At a ___ ___ ___ ___ ___ ___ ___ ___
       6   4   7

4. Where do you buy food?

   At a ___ ___ ___ ___ ___ ___ ___ ___ ___ ___
           11   3

B **Write the letters from Activity A. Answer the question.**

W <u>h</u> ___ ___ , ___ y ___ ___ ___ f ___ <u>v</u> ___ ___ <u>i</u> ___ <u>e</u>
  1 2 3   4   5 6 7   2 8 5 7 9 3 10

___ ___ <u>v</u> <u>i</u> ___ ?
11 5 8 9 10

It's _____.

C **Go online!**

1. Find a police station near your house. Go to www.google.com.

   Type [police station (your zip code)] .
   Click on [Search] .

2. Write the address and phone number of the police station.

   _____

Workbook Lessons	Workbook Pages	Student Book Pages
What's the matter?	110	159-160
My son is sick.	111	161
Health Problems and Remedies	112	162–163
I exercise.	113	164
Drink hot water.	114	165
Taking Medicine	115	166
Health Insurance	116	167
Grammar: Action Verbs and Negatives	117	168–169
Read: Lin and Ping	118	170
Write: My Health	119	171
Just for Fun	120	

A **Complete.**

| a cold | ~~a sore throat~~ | a stomachache |

1. <u>a sore throat</u>   2. _____   3. _____

B **Complete.**

| finger | foot | ~~hand~~ | leg |

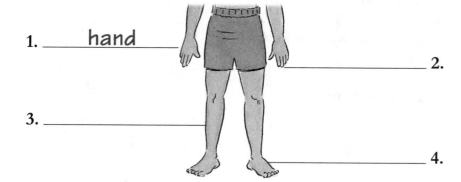

1. ___ hand ___

2. ___

3. ___

4. ___

C **Complete.**

| arm | headache | ~~matter~~ | with |

Mei: What's the _____ matter _____?

Eva: I have a _____.

Mei: What's the matter _____ Marco?

Eva: His _____ hurts.

A **Complete.**

| ~~bad~~ | doctor | need | stomach |

Ben: I feel _____**bad**_____. My

_____ hurts.

Alex: You _____ to see a

_____.

B **Complete.**

| fine | see | sick | ~~This~~ | Today |

Alex: Hello. _____**This**_____ is Alex Reyes. My son is _____. Can Dr. Black see him today?

Woman: Yes. Dr. Black can _____ him at 8:30.

Alex: _____ at 8:30? That's _____. Thank you.

C **Read Activity B. Complete.**

Ben's _____**stomach**_____ hurts. He has an appointment to see Dr. _____.

He will see the doctor _____ at _____.

A **Complete.**

> a cut   a cough   ~~a fever~~   an infection

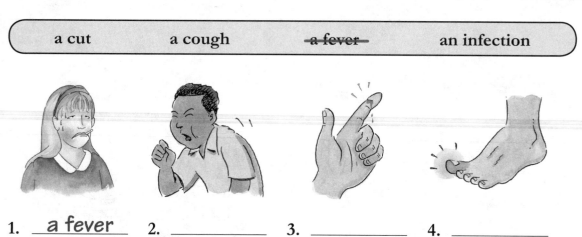

1. _a fever_   2. _____   3. _____   4. _____

B **Complete.**

> an antibiotic   ~~aspirin~~   a bandage   cough syrup

1. Ivan has a fever. He needs _____ aspirin _____.

2. Ly has an infection. She needs _____.

3. Mei has a cough. She needs _____.

4. Thomas has a cut. He needs _____.

C **Complete.**

> bad   bandage   ~~has~~   needs

David: Luna _____ has _____ a cut on her leg.

Eva: That's too _____. She

_____ a _____.

A **Match.**

1. ___C___ I exercise.

a.

2. _____ I drink a lot of water.

b.

3. _____ I don't eat junk food.

c.

4. _____ I get enough sleep.

d.

5. _____ I eat healthy food.

e.

B **Write what you do.**

I _____.

A **Complete.**

| cold | Rest | ~~have~~ | Drink |

Marco: I ___have___ a _____.

Lin: _____ orange juice.

Ivan: _____.

B **Complete.**

| shower | cough | Take | hot |

Eva: I have a _____.

Thomas: _____ a hot _____.

Aziza: Drink _____ water.

C **Complete.**

| stomachache | water | Drink | I |

David: _____ have a _____.

Luna: Rest.

Mei: _____ hot _____.

D **Write.**

Jane: I have a fever.

You: _____.

A Read.

THRIFTY DRUGSTORE

IVAN STOLI

3 DROPS IN EACH EAR

TWICE A DAY

THRIFTY DRUGSTORE
IVAN STOLI
3 DROPS IN EACH EAR
TWICE A DAY

THRIFTY DRUGSTORE

LUNA GILBERT

TAKE 1 PILL

TWICE A DAY

THRIFTY DRUGSTORE
LUNA GILBERT
TAKE 1 PILL
TWICE A DAY

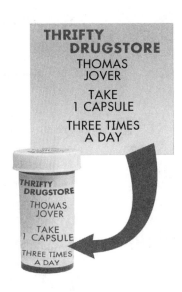

THRIFTY DRUGSTORE

THOMAS JOVER

TAKE 1 CAPSULE

THREE TIMES A DAY

THRIFTY DRUGSTORE
THOMAS JOVER
TAKE 1 CAPSULE
THREE TIMES A DAY

B Look at the pictures in Activity A. Circle.

Medicine for:	It's _____.			Take ____ a day.		
Ivan	a pill	a capsule	drops	1x	2x	3x
Luna	a pill	a capsule	drops	1x	2x	3x
Thomas	a pill	a capsule	drops	1x	2x	3x

A Read.

Lin has a health insurance card. She needs the card to see a doctor. Her health insurance is from her husband's work. Her husband's name is Hong.

Top Health Care Group

Name of Insured: **Lin Kwok**   ID#: **4769ALR**
Date of Birth: **4/19/66**   Plan: **Family**

Name of employee: **Hong Kwok**

Co-payment: **$15**   *Lin Kwok*

B Fill in the form for Lin.

Riverton Health Center

Patient's Name: Lin Kwok _____   Today's Date: _____

Date of Birth: _____

Name of Employee: _____

Type of plan: (circle one) individual   family

ID #: _____

Co-payment: YES/NO $_____

A Write the verbs in the correct form.

1. (walk) Alex _____ walks _____ every morning.

2. (play) Mei and Marco _____ soccer on Saturdays.

3. (read) I _____ every night.

4. (swim) Aziza and I _____ every day.

5. (run) You _____ every morning.

6. (drink) My dog _____ water.

7. (write) Luna _____ letters.

8. (lift weights) They _____ three times a week.

9. (walk) We _____ every day.

10. (run) Ly _____ on Sundays.

B Complete. Write the negative.

1. Mei likes bananas. Ivan _____ doesn't like _____ bananas.

2. I play basketball. Erik and Eva _____ basketball.

3. We eat chicken. They _____ chicken.

4. Thomas drinks milk. You _____ milk.

5. David dances. I _____.

6. Marco reads the newspaper. We _____ the newspaper.

7. Alex drinks orange juice. Luna _____ orange juice.

8. You like hamburgers. We _____ hamburgers.

9. I play soccer. Lin _____ soccer.

10. You eat junk food. I _____ junk food.

A **Read.**

Lin is 44 years old. Her mother Ping is 74 years old. Lin and Ping are healthy. They exercise every day. They like to walk in the park every day at 9:00 A.M. Once a week, Lin plays soccer. Ping dances once a week.

Lin and Ping eat healthy food. Lin likes carrots. Ping likes apples. They don't eat junk food and they don't smoke.

B **Complete.**

dances	eat healthy food	exercise every day
~~healthy~~	likes apples	likes carrots
44	plays soccer	walk in the park
74	don't eat junk food	don't smoke

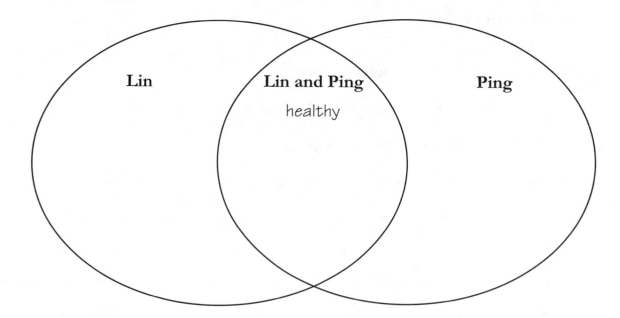

Lin   Lin and Ping   Ping

healthy

C **Write about you.**

1. I _____ every day.

2. I _____ once a week.

A Write what you do.

What I Eat	Exercises I Do
fruit	

B Look at Activity A. Circle the healthy things.

C Write the healthy things you do.

1. I _____.

2. I _____.

3. I _____.

D Write three healthy things you want to do.

1. I want to _____.

2. I want to _____.

3. I want to _____.

Just for Fun

A Circle the words.

ankle	arm	backache	cough	earache
fever	finger	foot	head	headache
infection	nose	sore throat	stomach	stomachache
toothache				

h	s	t	o	m	a	c	h	a	c	h	e	y	e	f
t	a	r	m	t	b	f	e	v	e	r	r	h	f	h
a	n	n	b	o	k	a	s	n	m	e	t	e	i	s
e	k	f	d	o	g	s	c	y	k	l	r	a	s	l
a	l	d	b	t	j	t	h	k	i	w	d	d	i	o
r	e	c	r	h	n	o	s	e	a	l	f	a	c	u
a	g	y	d	a	e	m	h	e	a	c	u	c	o	g
c	f	t	o	c	j	a	t	r	f	e	h	h	u	b
h	e	i	g	h	x	c	i	b	o	l	l	e	g	m
e	x	u	n	e	g	h	v	c	o	l	d	i	h	s
w	e	r	d	g	b	i	r	x	t	i	k	c	o	z
l	k	i	p	h	e	c	q	u	y	h	e	a	d	r
s	o	r	e	t	h	r	o	a	t	h	e	w	l	t
x	m	o	i	n	f	e	c	t	i	o	n	r	o

B Go online!

1. Find a drugstore in your city. Go to www.google.com.

   Type [drugstore (your zip code)].
   Click on [Search].

2. Bring the address and phone number for a drugstore in your city to class.

Workbook Lessons	Workbook Pages	Student Book Pages
What do you do?	122	175
A cook uses pots and pans.	123	176–177
I can drive.	124	178–179
Want Ads	125	180
I was a waiter.	126	181
A Paycheck	127	182
Safety Signs	128	183
Grammar: Simple Past of *Be* and *Can/Can't*	129	184–185
Read: Lin's Application	130	186
Write: A Conversation	131	187
Just for Fun	132	

A **Complete.**

| ~~cashier~~ | health aide | delivery person |
| computer programmer | waiter | sales clerk |

1. _cashier_   2. _____   3. _____

4. _____   5. _____   6. _____

B **Complete.**

| cook | ~~do~~ | I'm | person |

Erik: What ____do____ you do?

Mei: _____ a delivery _____. And you?

Erik: I'm a _____.

C **Write about you.**

Jane: What do you do?

You: I'm _____.

A **Match.**

1. __e__ a waiter
2. _____ a cook
3. _____ a sales clerk
4. _____ a computer programmer
5. _____ a construction worker

a. a cash register
b. a computer
c. tools
d. pots and pans
e. an order pad

B **Complete.**

1. An ____office worker____ uses a telephone.
2. A _____ uses an order pad.
3. A _____ uses a taxicab.
4. A _____ uses tools.
5. A _____ uses a computer.

C **Complete the chart.**

Jobs	Indoors	Outdoors	With People	With Machines
waiter	✔		✔	
sales clerk				
health aide				
delivery person				
taxi driver				

A **Complete.**

| drive | fix | ~~sell~~ | use |

1. ___sell___   2. _____   3. _____   4. _____

B **Complete.**

| And | computer | cook | ~~What~~ | you |

Aziza: ___What___ can _____ do?

Ly: I can _____. _____ you?

Aziza: I can use a _____.

C **Complete.**

| can't | car | fix | Yes | ~~you~~ |

Marco: Can ___you___ drive a _____?

Alex: _____, I can. Can you _____ things?

Marco: No, I _____.

D **Write about you.**

I can _____.

A Circle the jobs.

Can you drive?

Taxi driver
needed

6:00 P.M.–2:00 A.M.
Call (818) 555-0044

1

**WANTED:
Experienced
Computer
Programmer**

White Industries
1717 4th Street
San Diego, CA

Call Bob Miller
at (619) 555-9023

2

King Market

727 State Street
(415) 555-9929

Full-time cashier
needed.
$18/hour

3

B Match.

1. ___b___ Who do you call at White Industries?   a. 1717 4th Street

2. _____ What is the phone number at White Industries?   b. Bob Miller

3. _____ What is the address of King Market?   c. (818) 555-0044

4. _____ What is the phone number at Star Taxi Company?   d. 6:00 P.M.-2:00 A.M.

5. _____ What is the address of White Industries?   e. (619) 555-9023

6. _____ When is the taxi driver needed?   f. 727 State Street

C Read. Write the ad number from Activity A.

Lin: I was at Banana Computers for five years.

Eva: I was a cashier at a supermarket.

Thomas: I can drive a taxicab.

1. Lin: _____   2. Eva: _____   3. Thomas: _____

A **Write.**

before	do	were	taxi driver	~~was~~

Ivan: I _____ **was** _____ a sales clerk in Russia.

What did you _____ before?

Marco: I was a waiter in Colombia.

Ly and David: We _____ cooks in Vietnam.

What did you do _____?

Thomas: I was a _____ in Haiti.

B **Write about your family.**

1. My father was _____.

2. My mother was _____.

3. My _____.

4. _____.

C **Write about you.**

1. I was _____ in 1990.

2. I was _____ in 2000.

3. I was _____ in 2006.

A **Read.**

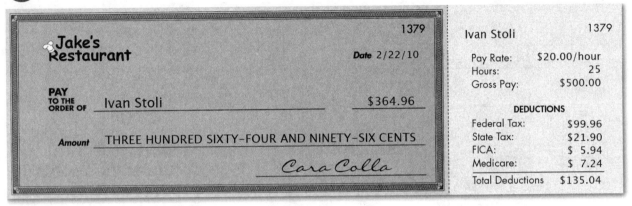

	1379
Jake's Restaurant	**Date** 2/22/10

PAY TO THE ORDER OF ___Ivan Stoli___ $364.96

Amount ___THREE HUNDRED SIXTY-FOUR AND NINETY-SIX CENTS___

Cara Colla

Ivan Stoli   1379

Pay Rate:	$20.00/hour
Hours:	25
Gross Pay:	$500.00

DEDUCTIONS

Federal Tax:	$99.96
State Tax:	$21.90
FICA:	$ 5.94
Medicare:	$ 7.24
Total Deductions	$135.04

B **Circle.**

1.	The paycheck is for _____.	(Ivan Stoli)	Cara Colla
2.	Ivan works at _____.	Jake's Restaurant	Cara Colla
3.	Ivan worked for _____.	20 hours	25 hours
4.	Ivan's take-home pay is _____.	$500.00	$364.96
5.	Ivan's federal taxes are _____.	$135.04	$99.96
6.	Ivan's state taxes are _____.	$21.90	$135.04

C **Write.**

1. Last week Ivan worked 25 hours. His gross pay was $_____.

2. His total deductions were $135.04. His take-home pay was $_____.

A Complete.

| Fire Extinguisher | Wash Hands | Emergency Exit |
| High Voltage KEEP OUT | Caution Work Area | No Smoking |

1. _____

2. _____

3. _____

4. _____

5. _____

6. _____

B Make a safety sign you see at school or work.

A **Write *was* or *were*.**

1. Alex and Luna ____were____ in Los Angeles last month.

2. I _____ a waiter in Brazil in 2005.

3. Aziza _____ a health aide in Somalia three years ago.

4. Yesterday Marco _____ at my house.

5. Thomas and I _____ in New York last week.

6. You _____ at work this afternoon.

7. Mei and David _____ in class this morning.

8. Eva _____ sick on Friday.

9. Eric _____ in Chicago in 2004.

10. Ly and Ivan _____ at the library yesterday.

B **Write *can* or *can't*.**

1. Ivan doesn't like to work with tools. He ___can't___ be a construction worker.

2. The post office is open. Mei _____ buy stamps.

3. Thomas likes to work with people. He _____ be a sales clerk.

4. Marco speaks Spanish and English. He _____ speak Vietnamese.

5. Jane likes to work with machines. She _____ be a construction worker.

6. Aziza likes to work with people. She _____ be a health aide.

7. David likes to work indoors. He _____ be a computer programmer.

8. Ly doesn't drive. She _____ be a taxi driver.

9. Luna doesn't like to work outdoors. She _____ be a delivery person.

10. Lin likes to fix things. She _____ be a construction worker.

What's your job? 129

Read: Lin's Application

A Read.

WHITE INDUSTRIES		
Human Resources		
Job Application		
Personal Information		
	Past	**Present**
Name	Lin Kwok	Lin Kwok
Address	Yong Road Beijing, China	474 Jones Street Troy, NY 12183
Telephone	–	(518) 555-6263
Education	Beijing Technical School	ESL Class City College

Job	**Employer**	**Dates**
Computer programmer	Banana Computers	2001–2006
Sales clerk	Kane's Department Store	1990–1997

Skills (Check what you can do.)

___✓___ Drive _✓___ car _____ van _____ truck

_____ Cook

___✓___ Use a computer

___✓___ Fix machines

Date: March 17, 2010   **Signature:** *Lin Kwok*

B Look at Activity A. Write the answers.

1. Where does Lin live now? _____ 474 Jones Street, Troy, NY _____

2. What is Lin's phone number now? _____

3. What was Lin's job from 1990–1997? _____

4. Who was her employer from 2001–2006? _____

5. Can Lin drive a truck? _____

6. Can she fix machines? _____

A **Complete the conversation. Use the sentences in the box.**

> I was a taxi driver in Haiti.
> Yes, it is. Thank you.
> I can work Tuesday to Saturday from 7:00 A.M. to 5:00 P.M.
> ~~I deliver refrigerators and stoves.~~
> Yes, I can.

Thomas wants a new job. He is calling Ms. Carter at United Delivery Company.

Thomas: Good morning, Ms. Carter. I'm calling about the want ad for a

delivery person. I work at Kane's Department Store now.

I deliver refrigerators and stoves. _____

Ms. Carter: What did you do before?

Thomas: _____ I can drive a car.

Ms. Carter: Can you drive a truck?

Thomas: _____

Ms. Carter: When can you work?

Thomas: _____

Ms. Carter: There is an opening from 7:00 A.M. to 2:00 P.M. Tuesday to Friday.
Is that good for you?

Thomas: _____

A **What are the words?**

Across →

2. I work in a store. I take money from people. I'm a _____.

3. I work in a restaurant. I give people food. I'm a _____.

Down ↓

1. I help sick people. I'm a _____.

2. I work in a restaurant. I make food. I'm a _____.

3. I answer phones and work with a computer. I'm an office _____.

B **Go online!**

1. Go to a search engine.

Type [jobs (your city)] .
Click on [Search] .

2. Write the website address for three job websites.

_____

_____

_____

Workbook Lessons	Workbook Pages	Student Book Pages
I take a bus.	134	191
It's straight ahead.	135	192–193
How do I get to the beach?	136	194–195
Getting a Learner's Permit	137	196
Road Signs	138	197
How often does the bus leave?	139	198
A Bus Schedule	140	199
Grammar: Questions with *Be, Do,* and *Does*	141	200–201
Read: An Appointment at School	142	202
Write: Getting to Work	143	203
Just for Fun	144	

I take a bus.

A Complete.

drive a car	walk	take a subway
take a bus	take a taxicab	ride a bike

1. ___drive a car___   2. _____   3. _____

4. _____   5. _____   6. _____

B Complete.

drive	~~ride~~	take	walk

Marco: How do you get to school?

Ivan: I ___ride___ a bike.

Thomas: I _____ a car.

Lin: I don't have a car. I _____.

Alex: I _____ a bus.

C Write about you.

Jane: How do you get to school?

You: _____.

A **Complete.**

> ahead   between   ~~me~~   post office   Where

David: Excuse ____ me ____. Where is the

_____?

Eva: It's straight _____.

Thomas: Excuse me. _____ is the restaurant?

Eva: It's _____ the drugstore and the library.

B **Look at the picture. Circle.**

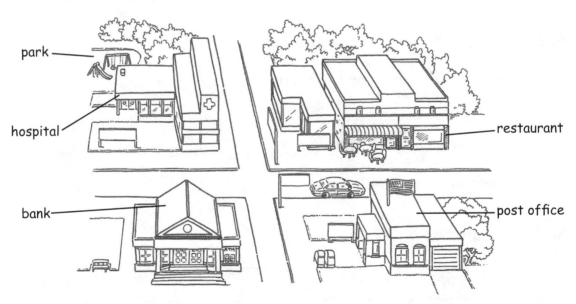

park

hospital

bank

restaurant

post office

1. Where is the hospital?   It's next to the bank.   (It's across from the bank.)

2. Where is the post office?   It's next to the bank.   It's across from the restaurant.

3. Where is the park?   It's next to the hospital.   It's next to the post office.

A **Match.**

1. __d__ J Train

2. _____ 12 Bus

3. _____ 47 Bus

4. _____ K Train

a. Downtown

b. Riverton Park

c. East Beach

d. Riverton Airport

B **Complete.**

Kim: How do I get to East Beach?

Thomas: Take the __12 Bus__.

Kim: How do I get _____ Riverton Airport?

Thomas: Take the _____.

C **Complete.**

7:30	does	next	Thanks

Aziza: When _____ *does* _____ the

_____ train to Dallas leave?

Woman: It leaves at _____.

Aziza: At 7:30? _____.

A **Read.**

Ivan: Hello. I want a learner's permit. Can I make an appointment for Tuesday?

Man: Yes. Can you come on Tuesday at 10:00?

Ivan: Tuesday at 10:00? That's fine.

Man: The test is $34.

Ivan: $34? Thank you.

B **Circle.**

1. Ivan wants _____.   a driver's license   (a learner's permit)

2. His appointment is on _____.   Tuesday   Thursday

3. His appointment is at _____.   10:00   3:00

4. The test is _____. $10 $34

C **Read. Complete the form.**

Ivan's full name is Ivan R. Stoli. His date of birth is September 6, 1982. His address is 174 Maple Street, Riverton, NY 14246. His phone number is (518) 555-6371.

Application for a Learner's Permit

1. Name: __Stoli_____
   (Last)   (First)   (MI)

2. Address: _____
            (Street)   (City)   (State)   (Zip)

3. Telephone: _____
              (Area Code)

4. Date of Birth: _____   5. ____ male ____ female
                  (MM/DD/YY)

6. Eye color: __blue_____   7. Hair color: __blond_____

A Complete.

| Bus Stop | ~~Hospital~~ | No Parking | One Way | Speed Limit | Stop |

1. <u>Hospital</u>

2. _____

3. _____

4. _____

5. _____

6. _____

B Circle the problem.

1.

2.

A Complete.

| does | every | hour | How | leave | minutes | often |

Marco: How often _____ does _____ the D Train leave?

Woman: It leaves _____ half hour.

Marco: Oh, good. At 2:00, 2:30, and 3:00.

Eva: _____ often does the subway leave?

Woman: It leaves every 15 _____.

Eva: Oh, good. At 12:00, 12:15, and 12:30.

Mei: How _____ does the bus

_____?

Woman: It leaves every _____.

Mei: Oh, good. At 6:00, 7:00, and 8:00.

B Circle.

1. 3:00   3:30   4:00   4:30   every hour   every half hour

2. 4:00   5:00   6:00   7:00   every hour   every half hour

3. 8:45   9:15   9:45   10:15   every half hour   every 15 minutes

4. 6:15   6:30   6:45   7:00   every half hour   every 15 minutes

5. 4:15   5:15   6:15   7:15   every hour   every 15 minutes

A **Read.**

WEEKDAYS	BUS 25 LEAVES			INBOUND
Beach Street	Riverton Park	Riverton Library	Westside Hospital	Riverton Airport
2:10	2:25	2:55	3:10	3:25
2:40	2:55	3:25	3:40	3:55
3:10	3:25	3:55	4:10	4:25
3:40	3:55	4:25	4:40	4:55
5:00	5:15	5:45	6:00	6:15

B **Look at the schedule in Activity A. Write.**

1. It's 3:20. When does the next bus leave Riverton Park? ___3:25___

2. It's 5:55. When does the next bus leave Riverton Airport? _____

3. It's 3:10. When does the next bus leave Riverton Library? _____

4. It's 4:05. When does the next bus leave Westside Hospital? _____

5. It's 3:31. When does the next bus leave Beach Street? _____

6. It's 3:20. Ivan is at Riverton Park. When does the next bus leave?

   _____

7. It's 5:30. Jane is at the library. When does the next bus leave? _____

8. It's 3:00. Eva is on Beach Street. When does the next bus leave? _____

9. It's 2:45. Marco is at the park. When does the next bus leave? _____

10. It's 4:14. Mei is at the airport. When does the next bus leave?

   _____

Grammar: Questions with *Be*, *Do*, and *Does*

A Write *what*, *where*, *when*, or *who*.

1. A: _____ When _____ is your class?   B: Tuesday mornings.

2. A: _____ is your school?   B: On Jones Street.

3. A: _____ is the teacher?   B: Jane Craft.

4. A: _____ is your class?   B: English.

5. A: _____ is the name of   B: City Adult School.
   your school?

6. A: _____ is your   B: Alex Reyes.
   classmate's name?

7. A: _____ is your classmate?   B: In class.

8. A: _____ is your classmate?   B: Ivan Stoli.

B Match.

1. __g__ How do you get to work?   a. She takes a bus.

2. _____ What train do you take?   b. She takes Bus 37.

3. _____ When does the train leave?   c. At 4:45.

4. _____ What time does the train arrive?   d. She gets it at the bus stop.

5. _____ How does Eva get to school?   e. It arrives at 8:45.

6. _____ Where does Eva get the bus?   f. I take the L Train.

7. _____ What bus does she take?   g. I take the train.

C Write about you.

Jane: What is the name of your school?

You: _____.

A **Read.**

7:00 A.M.

Ly is driving Jade to school. Jade usually takes the bus to school. Today Ly has an appointment with Jade's teacher. Ly's appointment is at 7:30. Jade's class starts at 8:00.

7:30 A.M.

Now Ly is talking to Jade's teacher. Jade is a good student. She does her homework every day. But there is a small problem. Jade sometimes talks to her classmates when the teacher is talking.

6:00 P.M.

Now Ly and Van are talking to Jade. They want Jade to stop talking to her classmates when the teacher is talking. Jade says O.K. Ly and Van are happy.

B ✔ **Check.**

What's a good title for this story?

_____ **1.** Jade's problem at school   _____ **2.** Ly drives Jade to school.

C **Answer the questions.**

1. How does Jade usually get to school? _____ *She takes the bus.*

2. What time is Ly's appointment? _____

3. What time is Jade's class?_____

4. Who does Jade talk to in class? _____

5. What do Ly and Van want? _____

A **Read.**

Getting to Work
by Mei Wu

In China, my family's house is near a restaurant. My sister lives in my family's house. She works at the restaurant. She walks to work every day.

In the US, I am a cook in a restaurant. I live far from my job. I take a train and a bus to work every morning. The train station is on Green Street. I take the M Train to 1st Avenue. Then I walk to my bus stop. My bus stop is on 2nd Avenue. I take the bus to 14th Avenue.

Some people at the restaurant walk to work. Some workers take the subway. Some workers drive. My boss Carol drives to work.

B **Write.**

Write a story. Answer these questions.
How do people get to work in your native country?
How do you and your classmates get to work now?

_____

_____

_____

_____

_____

_____

_____

A **Write the words.**

1. ___Take___ a bus.
   e k a T

2. _____ a bike.
   d R e i

3. _____ a car.
   r e v i D

4. _____ a subway.
   k a e T

5. _____ a train.
   k e a T

6. _____.
   k l a W

B **Go online!**

Find directions from your home to your school.

1. Go to www.maps.google.com.

   Type [(your address, city, state)].

   Click on [Search maps].

2. Click on **Get directions: <u>To here</u>**.

   Type [(the address of your school)].

4. Click [GO].

5. Print your map and bring it to class.

Correlation Tables

Unit 1

Student Book Pages	Workbook Pages
3	2
4	3
5-6	4
7	5
8-9	6
10-11	7
12	8
13	9
14	10
15	11
	12

Unit 2

Student Book Pages	Workbook Pages
19	14
20	15
21	16
22	17
23-25	18
26	19
27	20
28-29	21
30	22
31	23
	24

Unit 3

Student Book Pages	Workbook Pages
35-36	26
37	27
38-39	28
40	29
41	30
42	31
43	32
44-45	33
46	34
47	35
	36

Unit 4

Student Book Pages	Workbook Pages
55	38
56	39
57-58	40
59	41
60-61	42
62	43
63	44
64-65	45
66	46
67	47
	48

Unit 5

Student Book Pages	Workbook Pages
71	50
72-73	51
74-75	52
76	53
77	54
78	55
79	56
80-81	57
82	58
83	59
	60

Unit 6

Student Book Pages	Workbook Pages
87-88	62
89-90	63
91	64
92	65
93	66
94	67
95	68
96-97	69
98	70
99	71
	72

Correlation Tables

Unit 7

Student Book Pages	Workbook Pages
107	74
108-109	75
110-111	76
112	77
113	78
114	79
115	80
116-117	81
118	82
119	83
	84

Unit 8

Student Book Pages	Workbook Pages
123-124	86
125	87
126-127	88
128	89
129	90
130	91
131	92
132-133	93
134	94
135	95
	96

Unit 9

Student Book Pages	Workbook Pages
139	98
140	99
141	100
142-143	101
144-145	102
146	103
147	104
148-149	105
150	106
151	107
	108

Unit 10

Student Book Pages	Workbook Pages
159-160	110
161	111
162-163	112
164	113
165	114
166	115
167	116
168-169	117
170	118
171	119
	120

Unit 11

Student Book Pages	Workbook Pages
175	122
176-177	123
178-179	124
180	125
181	126
182	127
183	128
184-185	129
186	130
187	131
	132

Unit 12

Student Book Pages	Workbook Pages
191	134
192-193	135
194-195	136
196	137
197	138
198	139
199	140
200-201	141
202	142
203	143
	144

Photo Credits

Page 67 (4): © Don Farrall/Getty Images; 67 (all others): © The McGraw-Hill Companies, Inc./Ken Cavanagh Photographer; 79 (1): © The McGraw-Hill Companies, Inc./Jacques Cornell photographer; 79 (2): © The McGraw-Hill Companies, Inc./Ken Karp photographer; 79 (3): © Jonathan A. Nourok/PhotoEdit; 79 (4): © The McGraw-Hill Companies, Inc./Jacques Cornell photographer; 79 (5): © Ingram Publishing/Fotosearch; 79 (6): © The McGraw-Hill Companies, Inc./Jacques Cornell photographer; 87 (top left): © Tomi/PhotoLink/Getty Images; 87 (top right): © Photodisc/Getty Images; 87 (bottom left): © Ron Chapple/Thinkstock/Getty Images; 87 (bottom right): © Comstock/PunchStock; 91 (1): © image 100/Alamy; 91 (2): © Copyright 1997 IMS Communications Ltd/Capstone Design. All Rights Reserved; 91 (3): © Brand X Pictures; 91 (4): © Ryan McVay/Getty Images; 104 (all): © Kim Kulish/CORBIS; 115 (left): © Steven May/Alamy; 115 (middle & right): © Comstock/Alamy; 128 (1): © graficart.net/Alamy; 128 (2): © PhotoDisc/SuperStock; 128 (3): © Ablestock/Alamy; 128 (4): © Royalty-Free/CORBIS; 128 (5): © imagebroker/Alamy; 128 (6): © Michael Newman/PhotoEdit.